THE GOD OF EVOLUTION

The God of Evolution

A Trinitarian Theology

Denis Edwards

PAULIST PRESS
New York / Mahwah, N.J.

BT
712
.E3
1999

Cover image © Index Stock Imagery-Mauritius. Used by permission.

Cover design by Paz Design Group

Copyright © 1999 by Denis Edwards

Library of Congress Cataloging-in-Publication Data

Edwards, Denis, 1943–
    The God of evolution : a Trinitarian theology / by Denis Edwards.
        p.   cm.
    Includes bibliographical references (p.   ) and index.
    ISBN 0–8091–3854–9 (alk. paper)
    1. Evolution—Religious aspects—Christianity. 2. Trinity—History of doctrines. I. Title.
BT712.E3   1999
231.7'652—dc21   98–54244
                                                                          CIP

Published by Paulist Press
997 Macarthur Boulevard
Mahwah, New Jersey 07430

Distributed in Australia
by Word of Life Distributors/
Rainbow Book Agencies

www.paulistpress.com

Printed and bound in the
United States of America

Contents

Preface

THIS BOOK OWES A GOOD DEAL to the stimulation offered by a conference on biological evolution and divine action, cosponsored by the Center for Theology and the Natural Sciences (Berkeley) and the Vatican Observatory, which was held at Castelgandolfo, in June 1996. I have built on the paper I prepared for that conference, "Original Sin and Saving Grace in Evolutionary Context," which will appear in *Evolutionary and Molecular Biology: Scientific Perspectives on Divine Action*, edited by Robert John Russell, Francisco J. Ayala, and William R. Stoeger, S.J. (Vatican City State: Vatican Observatory Publications, and Berkeley, California: Center for Theology and the Natural Sciences, in press). I have also developed material that appeared in an article entitled "Evolution and the God of Mutual Friendship," which was published in *Pacifica* (1997): 187–200. Biblical quotations are from the New Revised Standard Version, copyright 1989, Division of Christian Education of the National Council of the Churches of Christ in the United States of America.

I am very grateful to colleagues and friends who have given precious time to reading the manuscript and who have made critical suggestions. They include theologians John Haught, Elizabeth Johnson, Mary Catherine Hilkert, Michael Trainor, Patricia Fox, and Christine Burke, and scientists Alistair Blake, Ian Gibbins, and Michele Grimbaldeston. My sincere thanks, too, to Kathleen Walsh and to all at Paulist Press.

1

1 Introduction: Evolution and God

THIS BOOK IS AN ATTEMPT TO RESPOND TO THE QUESTION: What difference does acceptance of the theory of evolution make to a Christian theology of God? If intellectual integrity demands that Christians accept the broad lines of the scientific account of biological evolution, what impact does this have on a Christian view of God?

Christian theology always needs to be done again. There is always the need to attempt to grasp the "good news of God" (Rom 1:1) from the perspective of a new cultural context. The evolutionary view of reality constitutes such a new context, one which is radically different from the contexts in which biblical, patristic, medieval, and reformation theologies were developed. A theology of God for today must attempt to be faithful to the insights of the "good news of God" from the context of an evolutionary view of the world. It must ask: How can we talk meaningfully of the Christian God in an evolutionary world? Attempting to answer this question involves what Ian Barbour has called a "theology of nature" and, more specifically, an attempt at what he calls a "reformulation" of Christian theology in the light of contemporary scientific insights.[1]

In this opening chapter, I begin by offering a brief summary of the evolutionary view that is broadly accepted in contemporary science. Then I turn to the accounts of creation that are found in the opening chapters of the Bible, attempting to distinguish what is simply a reflection of the worldview of ancient cultures and what has enduring importance for Christian theology.

The Evolutionary Worldview

Science tells us that the Earth, along with the rest of our solar system, was formed about four and a half billion years ago. Relatively soon afterward there was bacterial life on Earth. Scientists have discovered the remains of communities of microbes in rock formations that are more than three billion years old. They conclude that, by three and a half billion years ago, well-developed communities of bacteria were already spread around the Earth. These were the first ecosystems. Evidence from a number of disciplines leads to the conclusion that the whole pattern of life on Earth has evolved from these early communities of simple cells.

The contemporary evolutionary worldview has its origin in the work of Charles Darwin (1809–1882). Jean Baptiste de Lamarck (1744–1829) had already argued that creatures evolved by passing on characteristics that they acquired in adapting to different environments. Darwin, along with Alfred Russell Wallace, proposed that evolutionary change occurs not through passing on *acquired* characteristics, as Lamarck thought, but through passing on *inherited* characteristics. He argued that some inherited variations give an edge in successful adaptation to new environments. Darwin called this process by which inherited variations lead to better adaptation "natural selection."

The publication of Darwin's *On the Origin of Species* in 1859 marked the beginning of a new era in our understanding of the universe and of ourselves. Since the time of Copernicus and Newton it had been clear that the physical universe obeys laws of nature that account for the movements of planets as well as all the physical phenomena we experience on Earth. What Darwin offered was a way of understanding that *biological* life is also governed by natural laws. The diversity of organisms, the origin of species, even the origin of human beings, could now begin to be explained by an orderly process of change governed by laws that science could articulate and describe.[2]

Theologians like William Paley had long argued that the exquisite functional design of organs such as the eye proved the existence of a Creator. Darwin's theory proposed that even the emergence of finely tuned organs could be explained as the result of a natural process—natural selection. Natural selection could explain functional "design" without needing to appeal to an external divine designer. With natural selection, it was argued, the origin and adaptive nature of living organisms could be accounted for in terms of natural laws that operated within entirely natural processes.

At the heart of Darwin's theory is the insight that it is *inherited* variations that result in some creatures being better adapted than others to their environment and therefore more likely to leave more offspring. Darwin understood natural selection as the "preservation of favorable variations and the rejection of injurious variations."[3] He saw that some variations confer advantage in adapting to a particular environment and therefore to the possibility of survival. These advantageous variations would be transmitted to future generations more frequently on average than their alternatives. In time, favorable variations would be preserved and those that were not useful for adapting to a particular environment would be eliminated.

Darwin's theory suffered in that he had no way of accounting for the rise of inherited variations. Heredity was not well understood. But at the turn of the century, scientists began to absorb and adopt the insights on heredity that had already been developed by Gregor Mendel

(1822–1884). It became clear that inherited characteristics are transmitted across generations in units known as genes, and that these genes are inherited in a predictable fashion. It was discovered that changes in genes, called mutations, appeared to occur randomly. These mutations were now seen to be the source of novelty, which created the possibility of evolutionary change.

A number of early geneticists put the emphasis in their understanding of evolution on these mutations and neglected natural selection. Gradually it became clear that mutation and natural selection are both necessary to explain evolutionary change. But it was not until the 1930s that genetics and Darwinian natural selection were brought together in a satisfying synthesis, which Julian Huxley in 1942 named "the Modern Synthesis." This synthesis found expression in the work of scholars like Theodosius Dobzhansky and Ernst Mayr. In the following decades, zoology, paleontology, and botany all contributed to a revitalized Darwinism. In 1953, James Watson and Francis Crick discovered the double-stranded helical structure of deoxyribonucleic acid (DNA). For the first time it became possible to study evolution at the molecular level. Genetics and biochemistry were united to form molecular biology, which has provided a great deal of new evidence for reconstructing evolutionary history. The insights of molecular biology have been integrated within an expanded Darwinism to form a new synthesis.

There are many debates in modern biology. One example is the discussion over the degree to which evolutionary change can be attributed to natural selection and the degree to which it can be attributed to "neutral" change at the molecular level through genetic drift. The Japanese geneticist, Motoo Kimura, has argued that a great deal of change at the molecular level is "neutral" or random.[4] But this theory does not deny the role of natural selection in shaping the adaptive changes of organisms. Another issue in contemporary biology concerns the speed of evolutionary change. Stephen Jay Gould and Niles Eldredge have developed the theory of "punctuated equilibrium." They argue that, far from always evolving gradually and slowly, species tend to remain stable for long periods, and then these stable periods are "punctuated" by relatively rapid periods of change.[5] In spite of these and other areas of intense debate, it appears that the majority of biologists see the known data as consistent with a form of neo-Darwinism, in which genetic variation and natural selection are understood to be major factors in evolutionary change.

It is not the role of theology to enter into debates about the intricacies of evolutionary theory. But it is important for theology to enter into a critical dialogue with the broad picture offered by contemporary biology. This is the crucial theological question: How can we think about the Christian God if we take seriously the evolutionary worldview assumed by biological science?

The Biblical Stories of Origin

The Book of Genesis opens with stories of the origin of the world and of humankind in chapters 1–11, and then continues with the patriarchal narratives in chapters 11–50. These patriarchal narratives tell of the origin of the Hebrew people. While far from being history in the modern sense, these narratives, from Abraham and Sara onward, can be placed in the historical and cultural context of the Eastern Mediterranean world in the early part of the second millennium B.C.E. (2000–1500).[6]

7

The stories of origin in the first eleven chapters of Genesis have a very different character. They point to a primeval time, before human history, long before the time of Israel. They are not set in any specific place or related to historical events. The people in them have a larger-than-life character. The biblical stories of origin are told in the form of myths, which have parallels with other ancient myths such as the Enuma Elish creation myth and the Gilgamesh story from Babylon. In saying that some of these stories have a mythic character, I am simply describing their literary form. A story cast in mythic form may well be pointing to profound religious *truth*. But it should not be mistaken for anything like a modern historical or scientific account.

There are two stories of creation in the opening chapters of Genesis. The first is the well-known account of the creation of the world in seven days (1:1–2:4). This is followed by a second account of the creation of human beings set in the Garden of Eden (2:4–3:24).

Biblical scholars believe that the second account is by far the oldest. They think it comes from a preexisting source that they call the "Yahwist" source, so called because it uses the name *Yahweh* for God. This source may well have its origin in Judah, under King Solomon or one of his successors, in the late tenth or the ninth century B.C.E. It uses earthy language and vivid images. The Yahwist creation story begins with a bare earth and a stream welling up from the ground. In this context God, like a potter, forms the first human being from the clay, and breathes the breath of life into the earthling's nostrils. God then becomes a gardener, planting a garden in Eden and placing the human creature in it. God causes trees to grow, including the tree of life and the tree of the knowledge of good and evil. Because the human being is alone, God sets out to create a partner for the lonely individual.

From the ground God forms the wild animals and birds, but none of these turns out to be a suitable partner. So God finally takes one of the human being's ribs and builds it into a woman, and then, for the first time, there is genuine human companionship. Then follows the story of the eating of the forbidden fruit and the expulsion from the garden.

The first story of creation is very different. It is a carefully structured narrative, which places the creation of each kind of creature within a framework of seven days, culminating in the Sabbath. Many biblical commentators think that this account of creation comes from a much later source than the Yahwist narrative. They call it the "Priestly" source and suggest that it had its origin in or about the sixth century B.C.E. The Priestly account of origins gives a vast cosmic scope to God's work in creation. The whole universe and everything in it is created by God's word alone. All of creation is *good*. All living things receive their fertility from God and stand under God's blessing. The Priestly source stresses the dignity of human beings, made in God's image (Gn 1:27 and 9:6).[7]

In this Priestly account, the order of creation is as follows: the light, and with it day and night (first day); the dome of the sky separating the waters above from the waters below (second day); dry land and the sea, followed by plant life (third day); the sun, the moon, and the stars, set in the dome of the sky (fourth day); the fish, the sea creatures, and the birds (fifth day); the land animals and then humans (sixth day); God rests (seventh day). The creation of humans comes at the climax of this story. They are given "dominion" over other creatures, and they are told by God: "Be fertile and multiply; fill the earth and subdue it" (1:28). This is not to be construed as a license for the abuse of nature. Human beings are made in the divine image and

9

are to behave as God would behave.[8] The whole account leads to the joy, rest, and peace of the Sabbath.

What meaning do these texts have for a Christian theology today? As a theologian concerned about the doctrine of creation, I affirm that they do indeed have a great deal of meaning. But it is essential to distinguish between what has revelatory significance and what does not. The Second Vatican Council offered a fundamental criterion for interpreting the Bible when it pointed to the revelatory significance of the "truth for our salvation"[9] that is found in the biblical text. In reading the two Genesis accounts, it is helpful to distinguish the salvific truths they contain from the order of events of these stories and from the understanding of the physical universe that they take for granted. The salvific truths have revelatory significance for Christian theology today, but the historical order of events and the cosmology of the ancient world do not.

With regard to the *order of events*, it is essential to recognize that these stories are not an alternative to a contemporary scientific account. The biblical narratives are not authoritative in the area of the history of the early universe or the history of life on Earth. It is perfectly clear that the literary form of the first creation story is an artificial and pedagogical construct, aimed at teaching theological truth. The placing of human beings at the climax of the story and the placing of the Sabbath at the end indicates the importance of the dignity of the human before God, and the importance of the Sabbath as a sign of God's covenant blessing. The literary form of the second account is that of an ancient myth of origin. It has a completely different order of events from the first account. While in the first account God creates simply by the divine word, in the second God forms creatures like a potter, a gardener, and a surgeon. These two different accounts exist side by side, without embarrassment, and without any attempt to harmonize them. The point of the biblical stories is not the order of events or the time frame. In these primeval narratives, religious meaning is not attached to the historical order in which things occur, but to the theological insights that the narratives encapsulate. It is these theological insights that have significance for a Christian theology of creation.

In a similar way, the view of the natural world, or the *cosmology,* of these stories is not to be understood as authoritative for Christians today. The ancient peoples saw the inhabited word as emerging from and as completely surrounded by the "abyss" (Gn 1:2) of the primeval ocean. God creates a huge dome to separate the waters above us from the waters below us (Gn 1:7). At certain times, gates in the dome of the sky are opened, so that the water above us can come through to fall as rain on the ground. The water below us springs forth as fountains and rivers. God gathers the waters below the dome into a great basin, with the result that the sea is contained in the basin, while the dry land is safely separated from it (Gn 1:9). God attaches to the dome of the sky the great lights, the sun for the day, and the moon and stars for the night. A similar worldview was shared by many peoples in the ancient world. Needless to say, this is not the picture presented by science today. Again, it is important to affirm that a Christian of today can best learn about the evolutionary unfolding of the universe from science rather than from the Bible. The cosmology assumed by the biblical authors does not have authority for a Christian today. What have authority for today's Christian theology are the theological insights contained in the biblical narratives.

11

What, then, are these religious insights? It must be admitted that mythic narratives like those that open the Book of Genesis can say far more than can be put into propositional language. But, granted this, I would include the following among the "salvific truths" that I find communicated in these creation narratives: the preexistence and transcendence of God over all creatures; the ongoing relationship of all things to God as creatures to their Creator; God's delight in creatures; the divine proclamation of the goodness of creation; the blessing that makes creation fecund; the creation of human beings in the image of God; the call of the human being to work with creation but also to take care of it as God cares for it; the social nature of the human person; the insight that male and female represent the divine image; the goodness of human sexuality and marriage; the reality of human sinful rebellion against God, bringing alienation from God, from other human beings, and from creation itself; the enduring divine promise of salvation.

I regard these teachings of Genesis as a deep and profound heritage of the Jewish and the Christian communities. This is theological "truth for our salvation." It forms the context and framework for the trinitarian theology of the Creator God that will be developed in the chapters that follow. Of course, there is far more to a biblical theology of creation than the Book of Genesis. I have focused on the two narratives from Genesis, and tried to make plain the difference between revelatory truth and time-conditioned assumptions, because, for many people, there is an apparent conflict between Genesis and the theory of evolution. I hope that enough has been said to show that we should not look to Genesis for scientific teaching about the history of the early universe or the emergence of life. At the same time I hope it is clear that I advocate taking the religious insight and revelatory truth of these narratives with absolute seriousness. There is every reason for a Christian of today to embrace *both* the theological teachings of Genesis *and* the theory of evolution. But holding together the Christian view of God and the insights of evolutionary science does demand a rethinking of our theology of the trinitarian God at work in creation. This is what I take up in the chapters that follow.

2   *The God of Evolution as a God of Mutual Friendship*

IF CHRISTIANS ARE TO ACCEPT THE WORLDVIEW offered by contemporary science, that the universe unfolded over the last fifteen billion years from a primeval Big Bang, and that life evolved on Earth over the last three and a half billion years by means of genetic mutation and natural selection, then they come face to face with the question: How do these insights relate to the Christian concept of God?

Of course, there are those who find no need to be concerned about this interrelationship. On the one hand, there are a number of scientifically trained people who assume that the explanations offered by evolutionary biology simply rule out any need for a Creator. On the other hand, there are Christians who take such a literal view of biblical faith that they exclude the insights offered by biological evolution.

But there are also people like myself, who find both these positions shortsighted and arbitrary, and who look for a way to hold together the best insights of biology and Christian theology. Taking this stance requires a theological approach that can show that it is reasonable, coherent, and enlightening to hold both sets of insights together in one unified view. The central issue concerns the theological conception of God. What does saying yes to evolution mean for a theology of God? How can we think of the God of Jesus of Nazareth as a God who creates through a process that involves random mutation and natural selection? What kind of theology of God is faithful to both biblical faith and contemporary scientific insights and is capable of integrating both?

14

Step
A)

The God of Mutual Relations

In this section, I suggest that the foundation for a theology that takes evolution seriously can be found in the trinitarian vision of God as a God of mutual relations, a God who is communion in love, a God who is friendship beyond all comprehension. One could develop this theology from a variety of biblical and theological sources. I discuss only two, the theology of mutual relations at the heart of John's Gospel and Richard of St. Victor's theology of the Trinity.

Before attempting to develop this "mutual relation" approach to God, it might be helpful to situate it in the context of recent approaches to evolutionary theology that concentrate on God as the principle of "altruism." Writers such as Gerd Theissen and Philip Hefner have focused their attention on the connection between biological and cultural evolution, and on the emergence of altruistic or self-sacrificing love. They see the evolution of altruism as grounded in the fundamental character of reality, which they identify with God. Philip Hefner writes that the Christian claim is that "altruistic love holds the status of a cosmological and ontological principle."[1] While I find much to learn in the work of Theissen and Hefner, I suggest, by contrast, that it is not altruism, but the love of mutual relations that has this status.

It is undeniable that the Gospel calls for love of the "other" and that the cross of Jesus is the central Christian symbol of self-sacrificing love. Altruism is clearly a radical dimension of the Christian understanding of divine and human love. But is altruism a sufficient description of this love? There are two reasons why I think it better to look beyond altruism to express the ultimate Christian vision of the reality that is behind our evolutionary history.

The first reason comes from theological anthropology.

Feminist scholars have argued that Christian theologies of sin and salvation show the effect of having been constructed by men. In traditional theology, there has been a tendency to identify sin with pride, self-assertion, and self-centeredness. But does this reflect universal human experience? The theological admonition to a more self-sacrificial love may well offer a corrective to a dominant form of sinfulness operative in powerful people, but it may exacerbate an oppressed person's sin of "hiding" from freedom and self.[2] Altruism may be essential learning for dominant groups, but some oppressed persons may be thought of as "altruistic" to a fault. Admittedly this latter form of altruism does not represent the Christian concept, which involves self-love as well as love of the other. But the point is that, in some circumstances, indiscriminate calls to altruism and self-sacrifice can function to maintain oppression. This argument, in my view, does not undermine the significance of the sacrificial love of the cross, nor the importance of altruistic love, but offers an important critique of indiscriminate, undifferentiated, and uncritical calls to self-sacrifice and altruism.

The more fundamental reason for reserve about the ultimacy of altruism comes not from anthropology but from the doctrine of God. From the perspective of trinitarian theology, I will suggest that, even while the cross of Jesus points to altruism and self-sacrifice as essential components of divine and human love, love is revealed most radically in the trinitarian relations of mutual, equal, and ecstatic friendship. The Christian ideal of love is undeniably altruistic, but it is more than altruistic. It concerns self-possession as well as self-giving, love of self as well as love of the other. In Christian trinitarian theology, altruism is understood within a vision of mutual and equal relations. So, while Philip Hefner sees altruistic love as holding the status of "a cosmological and ontological principle," I believe that it is Persons-in-Mutual-Relations that has this status.

The Gospel of John

The good news of Christianity is that God is not simply a God of self-sacrifice, but a God of reciprocal giving and receiving, a God of mutual trinitarian love. It is obvious that the Christian Scriptures do not, and could not, contain the fully developed trinitarian theology that was to emerge in the fourth century. However the foundations for such a theology can be found in Paul's concept of our participation in divine life (Gal 4: 4–8; Rom 8:10–18), as well as in the baptismal and transfiguration scenes of the Synoptic Gospels and the final commission in Matthew's Gospel (Mt 28:9). But it is in the theology of John that we find the most developed theology of a threefold divine presence: a presence to the disciples of the "Paraclete," a return of Jesus himself to the disciples, and a presence to the disciples of "the Father" along with Jesus.

In John, the disciples are presented as caught up in the dynamic union of the mutually shared divine life. This shared life is expressed by the author in a variety of ways. One way is through the Johannine notion of reciprocal *abiding*. John uses the Greek words *menein en* to describe the "abiding in" one another that holds together the Father and the Son and Christian believers. This can be translated as "abide in," "remain in," "stay in," or "dwell in." The word *menein* is used forty times in John's Gospel, twenty-seven times in the Johannine letters, and only twelve times in the other three Gospels. John also uses the verb *einai en* ("to be in") with the same meaning. The word *abiding* has the profound theological meaning of divine "indwelling" in some

17

texts, and apparently a more ordinary sense of "remaining with" in others. But, of course, in John's Gospel, even this ordinary usage can have deeper theological resonances.[3]

At the beginning of the Gospel, John the Baptist testifies: "I saw the Spirit descending from heaven like a dove, and it *abided* on him. I myself did not know him, but the one who sent me to baptize with water said to me, 'He on whom you see the Spirit descend and *abide* is the one who baptizes with the Holy Spirit'" (1:32–34). Jesus is understood as someone on whom the Spirit abides permanently and as someone who then acts in the power of the Spirit.

The first disciples are presented as asking Jesus: "Where are you *abiding?*" He responds: "Come and see." Then we are told that they "came and saw where he was *abiding* and they *abided* with him that day" (1:38–39). The message is abundantly clear. We are to understand that discipleship is about abiding with Jesus. In John 4, where we find Jesus presented as the one who brings living water, we are told that Jesus *abides* with the Samaritan villagers for two days (4:40). In John 6, which is devoted to Jesus as the bread of life, we are told that Jesus will give us the food that *abides* to eternal life (6:27). In this same chapter, Jesus promises a mutual abiding: "Those who eat my flesh and drink my blood *abide* in me and I in them" (Jn 6:56). In John 8, we hear that true discipleship means abiding in Jesus' word: "If you *abide* in my word, you are truly my disciples; and you will know the truth and the truth will make you free" (8:31).

In John 14, we come to a highly developed concentration on the theme of a threefold divine abiding in the disciples. First, at the beginning of the chapter, we read: "In my Father's house there are many *abiding places;* if it were not so, would I have told you that I go to prepare a place for you?" (14:2). A few verses later, Jesus replies to Philip's request to see the Father: "Do you not believe that I am in the Father and the Father is in me? The words that I say to you I do not speak on my own; but the Father who *abides* in me does his works. Believe me that I am in the Father and the Father is in me" (14:10–11). Then we move to a theology of the divine indwelling in the disciples. Three times we find repeated the condition that the disciples are to love Jesus and keep his commandments (vv. 15, 21, 23); then, each time, there is a promise that a divine presence will come to dwell in those who practice this love. In verses 15–17, we hear of the giving of the *Paraclete:* "And I will ask the Father, and he will give you another Advocate, to be with you forever…. You know him, because he *abides* with you, and he will be in you." In verses 18–20 we hear of the coming back of *Jesus:* "I am not leaving you orphaned; I am coming back to you…. On that day you will know that I am in my Father, and you in me, and I in you." In verses 23–24 we hear of the coming of *the Father* with Jesus, both of whom will abide with the disciples: "Those who love me will keep my word, and my Father will love them and we will come to them and make our *abiding place* with them" (14:23).

The theme of the disciples' abiding in Jesus appears in its most highly developed form in John 15, with the image of the vine and branches: "*Abide* in me as I *abide* in you. Just as the branch cannot bear fruit by itself unless it *abides* in the vine, neither can you unless you *abide* in me" (15:4). Because Jesus is the vine and we are the branches, we are told: "Those who *abide* in me and me in them bear much fruit, because apart from me you can do nothing" (15:5). Whoever does not abide in Jesus is thrown away like a dead branch (15:6). The disciples are told: "If you *abide* in me and my words *abide* in you, ask for whatever you wish, and it will be done for you" (15:7). Then the theme is summarized in terms of abiding in Jesus' love as he abides in the Father's love: "As the Father has loved me, so I have loved you; *abide* in my love. If you keep my commandments, you will *abide* in my love, just as I have kept my Father's commandments and abide in his love" (15:9–10). Abiding in Jesus' love demands loving one another as Jesus has loved us (15:12, 17). While the vine and branch image refers primarily to the relationship between Jesus and the disciples, it also points to the love between disciples. Those who practice this love are called *friends:* "You are my friends if you do what I command you.... I do not call you servants any longer...but I have called you friends" (15:14–15).

These reciprocal relationships appear again in the great prayer of John 17, in terms that are equivalent to the language of mutual abiding. Jesus prays:

> That they may all be one. As you, Father are in me and I am in you may they also be in us, so that the world may believe that you have sent me. The glory that you have given me I have given them, so that they may be one, as we are one, I in them and you in me, that they may be completely one, so that the world may know that you have sent me and have loved them even as you have loved me.... I have made your name known to them, and will make it known, so that the love with which you have loved me may be in them, and I in them. (17: 21–25)

According to John, the love of Jesus and the Father in the Spirit, is a dynamic relational life of mutual indwelling, which reaches out to embrace us, catching us up in the open circle of divine love. In 1 John we are told simply that "God is love" (4:8, 16). This early Christian theology is very much concerned with the divine mutual indwelling with human beings, and more specifically with disciples. But once such a trinitarian and relational view of God emerged it could be applied not only to the life of grace, but also in a different way to the divine presence to all things in the relationship of ongoing creation.

Richard of St. Victor

The Greek Christian tradition came to understand this divine love as a circle of *koinōnia* (communion) and of *perichōrēsis*. *Perichōrēsis* is a word used by John Damascene (675–749) to describe the being-in-one-another, the mutual dynamic indwelling of the trinitarian Persons.[4] It comes from *perichōrēo*, meaning to encompass, and it describes reciprocal relations of intimate communion. The word suggests a communion in which diversity and unity, rather than being opposed, are understood as directly related to each other. It points to a unity in which individuality and diversity find full expression in interrelationship with others. Perichoresis expresses the ecstatic presence of each Person to the others, the being-in-one-another in supreme individuality and freedom. It points to a relationship in which each Person is present to the other in a joyous and dynamic union of shared life.

I find a particularly rich insight into this communion in the work of the Western theologian, Richard of St. Victor (d. 1173) and particularly in his concept of the mutual love of friends as a way of understanding the trinitarian relations.[5] Richard sees the self-transcending love of friendship as the high point of human life and argues that such friendship must be found in God. Because he cannot accept that the fullness of love is self-love, Richard cannot be content with a theology that sees God simply as loving Godself. Real friendship is love which goes from the self to the other.

Richard is sometimes accused of attempting to "prove" the doctrine of the Trinity. But he clearly begins his thinking from the trinitarian faith of the church. What he does offer, in this context of the living faith of the believing community, is a defense of the reasonableness of the doctrine of the Trinity. I believe that his arguments have particular value today. Part of the inheritance of the Enlightenment, and part of the experience of modernity, is that there has been a tendency to dismiss the Trinity as unbelievably mythological. To some, it seems more credible to believe in a more or less unitarian God, who is present to different modes. I believe that this modern form of "modalism" needs a response and that part of this response can be put in terms worked out by Richard of St. Victor. He would say to us today: If we accept that relationality is fundamental to our experience of life in the world, must not this relationality be grounded in the divine life? If friendship and interpersonal love (understood as self-transcending love) is the deepest and most important experience we have as human beings, must not we suspect that this reflects something that is in God?

Richard argues that if God is supreme in goodness, happiness, and glory, then there must be in God the supreme expression of self-transcending and mutual love. If there is to be this kind of mutual love in God, then it is obvious that there must be in God more than one Person; there must be at least two. Such love between divine Persons would need to be understood as radically equal and mutual. It would involve necessarily a self-transcending love that is eternally mutual.

In Richard's theology, the limited human experience of union in friendship points to the infinitely more profound unity of the divine communion. Divine unity must involve the divine Persons sharing equally from all eternity. The love shared by the trinitarian Persons would be so mutual and so equal that their unity would be beyond human comprehension—the unity of the divine substance or nature. The human experience of unity in love gives us only a faint and inadequate glimpse into the unity of this kind of trinitarian love.

But Richard's insight into friendship leads him to suggest that real love does not remain with the two but wants to share love with another. For full love we look for one who can share our love for the beloved. Richard sees the friendship in the Trinity as ecstatically breaking out beyond the two to include a third, whom he calls the *condilectus*. This word means literally the "one who is loved with" another. It had been translated as "a common friend."[6] There is no sense in which this common friend is loved any less than the other two. In the love of the divine Persons, Richard sees supreme love flowing equally in all directions.

Richard's theology suggests that it is friendship which is at the heart of things. I find this a fruitful way to approach an understanding of the God of evolution. This idea appears in contemporary feminist theology in different ways. Sallie McFague, for example, offers the image of God as Friend of the universe, and she sees human beings as creatures called into friendship with the Friend of the universe.[7] Elizabeth Johnson portrays the divine economy in terms of trinitarian friendship: the Spirit befriends us, making us friends of God; Jesus-Sophia is the incarnation of divine friendship inviting us to table and calling us to be not servants but friends (Jn 15:5); and "the creative love of Mother Wisdom reaches throughout the universe and all of its embedded individual lives with a friendship brimming with desire for the well-being of the whole of her creation."[8] Johnson states that "the love of friendship is the very essence of God."[9]

The claim that the divine life can be understood in terms of friendship must be understood, like all such claims about God, as analogical language, in which a fundamental negation and qualification are always implied. In this case, the negation and qualification mean that mutual friendship in God is not to be understood simply as limited human friendship, but as mutual love which *infinitely* transcends all notions of human friendship. But granted this, I believe that it is profoundly accurate to say that "the love of friendship is the very essence of God."

If this affirmation is taken seriously, then it means that mutual friendship is the fundamental principle from which all creatures spring. It is not only Richard of St. Victor, of course, who sees relations of mutual love as central to the Christian view of God. This idea is found in all the great mainstream Christian theologies of God, including the different theologies of the Cappadocians in the East and Augustine and Aquinas in the West. But it is Richard who develops the image of mutual love on the analogy of human friendship. For him, it is friendship that enables all creatures to be and to become. And along with other trinitarian theologians, he provides a foundation for seeing the "cosmological and ontological" principle of the universe as personal, relational, and communal.

The Fundamental Character of Reality as Relational

This relational view of God is a point of contact with biological science, which understands reality as an interdependent, relational process. In a biological worldview, things are interconnected and interrelated at all levels, whether it be the level of the cell, the organism, the ecosystem, or the

24

planetary community. The evolution of life is understood in communal and interactive terms.

An example of this is Lynn Margulis's widely accepted theory of the origin of mitochondria. Mitochondria are tiny bodies, which exist in thousands in each of our cells. In the membranes of these mitochondria, energy from food molecules is stored and released for use in a controlled way. Margulis has argued that the ancestors of mitochondria are the prokaryotic (cells without a nucleus) bacteria that already inhabited the Earth two billion years ago and still dominate life on Earth today. Offspring of these bacteria are assembled with other bacteria to inhabit larger eukaryotic cells (cells with a nucleus), which make up our bodies. Each of these cells is, then, a community of the descendants of these ancient bacteria. Richard Dawkins comments on this:

Each one of us is a community of a hundred million million mutually dependent eukaryotic cells. Each one of those cells is a community of thousands of specially tamed bacteria, entirely enclosed within the cell, where they multiply as bacteria will. It has been calculated that if all the mitochondria in a single human body were laid end to end, they would girdle the Earth, not once but two thousand times. A single animal or plant is a vast community of communities placed in interacting layers, like a rain forest. As for a rain forest itself, it is a community seething with perhaps ten million species of organisms, every individual member of every species being itself a community of communities of domesticated bacteria.[10]

Dawkins tells us that he finds this vision of the cell as an enclosed garden of bacteria, more inspiring, exciting, and uplifting than the story of the Garden of Eden. One can share Dawkins's wonder at this picture without necessarily sharing his generally negative attitude to biblical faith. In fact, as I hope I am making clear, I find this communal picture of the evolution of life beautifully congruent with the way a communal, relational God might create.

What I suggest in this chapter is not only that there is a congruence between the theological view of God as a God of radical friendship and the biological understanding of the interrelational nature of all living things. I want to go further to suggest that the notion of God's being as radically relational suggests that reality is *ontologically* relational. The very *being* of things is relational being. Ontology refers to the study of the fundamental nature of reality, to the study of being itself. Once the nature of God is understood as relational, then this suggests that the fundamental nature of all reality is relational.

I have been arguing, from the theology of God found in John's Gospel and Richard of St. Victor, that God's being is relational and interpersonal—that God is a God of mutual friendship. And if God's being is relational being, then what God creates can be understood to exist only in relation to the creator as relational being. This insight is supported by a number of theologians who are engaged in the late twentieth-century retrieval of the doctrine of the Trinity. The Orthodox theologian John Zizioulas, for example, points back to the intellectual breakthrough made by the Cappadocians, Basil the Great (c. 330–379), Gregory of Nazianzus (330–389) and Gregory of Nyssa (330–395) in the theology of the trinitarian God. Their insight, he says, is that "the being of God is a relational being." Zizioulas tells us that God's being *is* communion. This communion is a "primordial ontological concept," not a notion added to the divine substance, or something that follows substance.[11] Thus, Zizioulas argues, communion rather than substance is the fundamental ontological concept. It is communion that makes things be. Nothing exists without it. Reality springs from Persons-in-Relation. "God" has no ontological content without communion. Nothing is conceivable as existing only by itself. There is no true being without communion.[12]

The German theologian Walter Kasper follows Richard of St. Victor in developing his own theology of God as a "communion in love." He understands the unity of the divine nature as a "unity in love." This view of God leads Kasper to a relational view of reality as such. It suggests a "breaking out of an understanding of reality that is charac-terized by the primacy of subject and nature, and into an understanding of reality in which person and relation have priority."[13] In a similar way, Catherine LaCugna sees not only God but also created reality as fundamentally rela-tional and personal. She writes that "God's To-Be is To-Be-in-relationship, and God's being-in-relationship-to-us *is* what God is."[14] Her trinitarian theology becomes a sus-tained argument for what she calls an ontology of relation. So she writes that an ontology that is proper to the God of the economy of salvation "understands being as being-in-relation not being-in-itself."[15]

This ontological insight, that reality is relational because God is Persons-in-Relation, provides the foundation for building a theology of God that takes account of biological evolution. It provides the basis for a vision of the funda-mental reality of the universe as relational. It provides a theological foundation for seeing life on Earth as an interre-lated biological community, dependent upon a God who is Persons-in-Mutual-Love.

If the essence of God is relational, if the very foundation of all being is relational, if everything that is springs from Persons-in-Relation, then I would argue that this points toward a fundamental understanding of created reality which might be called an ontology of "being-in-relation." In such an understanding of reality, not only is God Persons-in-Relation, but each creature can be understood as a being-in-relation.[16]

Of course, there is an infinite difference between created being-in-relation and the divine communion. But what continuous creation means is that created being-in-relation always springs from, depends upon, and in a creaturely way participates in, the being of divine Persons-in-Relation.[17]

This theological view of the fundamental character of reality fits with key insights of evolutionary biology. Biology suggests a world of cooperative, coadaptive, symbiotic and ecological relations. Along with other areas of twentieth-century science, it supports a view of nature that is fundamentally relational. Biology and theology both point toward a view of reality in which relationships have a primary place. Trinitarian theology and ecological biology can meet in an ontology, which understands the being of things as being-in-relation.

The God of trinitarian theology is a God of mutual and equal relations. When such a God creates a universe it is not surprising that it turns out to be a radically relational and interdependent one. When life unfolds through the process of evolution, it emerges in patterns of interconnectedness and interdependence that "fits" with the way God is.

Creation Unfolding "Within" God

In this attempt at a theology that makes sense in the light of Christian revelation and biological evolution, I have suggested so far that a central and foundational concept is that God is a relational God, a God of equal and mutual friendship, and that all of created reality is to be understood as relational. To be is to be in communion. At the most fundamental level, being *is* communion.

If it is accepted that God is communion, and that the universe itself is a created communion existing from the divine communion, then this raises the question of how we think about the relationship between the divine communion and the community of creatures. We cannot think about this relationship without some kind of imaginative picture of God's interaction with the universe.

It is a central tenet of, and condition for, Christian theology that God transcends all our concepts and all our imaginative constructs. Yet, if we are to think of God and speak of God, we must use images and concepts. The only solution is a critical awareness of the limits of our words and mental pictures. What is needed is awareness that all our ways of imaging God are inadequate. When we come to think of God's "place" in relation to the universe, we need to acknowledge that our imaginations and our concepts are necessarily misleading. God is not contained by space, yet God is present and active in every part of what we know as space. Furthermore, words like *place, contained, present,* and *active* are words taken from everyday experience in the world and applied to God in an analogous fashion. This means that when we use them, we need to be aware of the ways in which they do *not* apply to a transcendent God, and of the ways in which what we affirm by them is true of God in a way that is *beyond* all creaturely limits.

We necessarily locate God in our images and concepts. Even though we know today that space-time unfolds from the Big Bang, with the emergence of the universe itself, and even though we know God radically transcends all our notions of space and time, yet still we imaginatively place

God somewhere in relation to the universe. I would argue that some ways of thinking about God's place in relation to creation are less inadequate than others, and part of theology's role is to point to ways of envisaging this location that are as faithful as possible to the best insights of science and the Christian tradition. The old popular idea of God as located in the heavens, understood as the sky, is clearly no longer viable in a world of the Hubble telescope and space travel. But there is another common imaginative picture, held I think, quite unreflectively, by many believers and unbelievers alike: God (usually as a unipersonal individual being) and the universe are understood as two realities, more or less over against each other, with God reaching into the world to act at particular moments. This common way of imaging the God–world relationship results in an interventionist view of divine action. God is imagined as intervening to create and to move creation in the right direction at certain times.

I argue for another image that is also necessarily inadequate, but which is less inadequate than those described above. *The universe can be understood as unfolding "within" the trinitarian relations of mutual love.* Creation takes place and flourishes within the divine life. The events of creation and redemption through the death and resurrection of Christ can be understood as taking place within the eternal dynamic life of the divine Persons. Hans Urs von Balthasar is one who has adopted this approach. He writes: "It is the drama of the 'emptying' of the Father's heart, in the generation of the Son, that contains and surpasses all possible drama between God and a world. For any world only has its place within that distinction between Father and Son that is maintained and bridged by the Holy Spirit."[18] For von Balthasar, every drama that can be played out in creation is

30

already contained in and surpassed in the eternal "event" of inner trinitarian love whereby the Father begets the Word. The begetting of the Word is an eternal act of letting go, of divine *kenosis*, of creating space for the other. Von Balthasar speaks of God's action in creation and redemption as "the play within the play."[19] Our play, the drama of creation and redemption, plays within the larger play of the divine life. The drama of divine action in creation takes place within the drama within the trinitarian life of God.[20]

What I am suggesting, then, is that the "place" of the universe is *within* God. The shared divine life is the ambience in which the universe is brought to life and enabled to unfold. This shared divine life must be understood as endlessly dynamic. In this life of God, the one who is Matrix and Source, Mother and Father, eternally gives self away in love in the act of begetting the one who is Wisdom and Word, and this springing forth of divine life eternally transcends itself ecstatically in the one who is Holy Spirit. The divine Persons are united eternally in what can be called the "play," and which can also be thought of as the "dance" of mutual perichoretic love. Creation, including the evolution of life, occurs within the "space" of this divine life.

Creation can be understood as the self-expression of the Trinity, whereby the divine Persons-in-Relation make space for what is not God within the divine life. It is the free expression of the fecundity of the divine life. I find the theology of Bonaventure (1221–1274) a rich resource for a contemporary theology of creation.[21] He sees creation as the free ecstatic overflow of the fecundity of the divine trinitarian love. He sees the first Person of the Trinity as the "Fountain Fullness" *(fontalis plenitudo)* and as the origin of all fecundity.[22] The eternal Word is the self-expression of this divine fecundity within the Trinity. As such the Word is also the Exemplar for all creatures. Within the Trinity the Word is the image of the Fountain Fullness, and with regard to creation the Word is the exemplar and eternal art *(ars aeterna)* for the creation of everything that comes into existence.[23] Everything that comes to be is created in divine Wisdom through the ecstatic and fecund Spirit of God.

The becoming of the world is grounded in the eternal trinitarian process. There is no necessity which demands that God have a world, since love is realized and expressed in the perichoresis of the divine Persons. But the three Persons share an infinite "space" of divine life, a space of dynamic giving and receiving, of infinitely playful invention and exploration. Within this space the divine Persons freely make room for the otherness of finite creatures.

Jurgen Moltmann has said that the trinitarian relationship of the divine Persons is "so wide the whole creation can find space, time and freedom in it." He suggests, rightly in my view, that we need to think of the creation of the universe as involving a "withdrawal" of God to make space for creation.[24] God makes space for the emergence of a universe and for the evolution of living creatures. Elizabeth Johnson agrees with these insights and points out: "To be so structured that you have room inside yourself for another to dwell is quintessentially a female experience." She points out that every human being " has lived and moved and had their being inside a woman, for the better part of the year it took for them to be knit together."[25] I find this experience of a mother making space in the womb for another a wonderfully rich and evocative image for the divine generativity by which the universe is brought forth within God.

Evolution is in God, within the trinitarian relations, expressing the ecstatic fecundity of this love. But it is also equally true to say that *the trinitarian God is in creation and pre-*

sent to every creature. God is radically interior to everything God creates, enabling it to be and to become. The God of mutual relations is the God of continuous creation. Continuous creation is itself a relation, the interior relation between each creature and God by which the creature exists. "Reality is intrinsically relational," Stephen Happel writes, "because God is present as inner relationality."[26] The relation of creation means that the transcendent God, Persons-in-Mutual-Communion, is immanent to every creature, with a wonderfully differentiated interior relation to each of them, constantly luring each to be and become. As Bill Stoeger puts it, "God acts immanently in nature—in every 'nook and cranny' of nature, at the core of every being and the heart of every relationship—to constitute and maintain it just as it is and just as it evolves."[27] And from the side of the creature, this relationship is the creature's own finite and specific participation in God's own trinitarian relationships.

This relationship between God and each creature is not yet what it will be when "all things" will be transformed in Christ (Col 1:20). According to the biblical promises, the universe is not yet what it will be, because it is not yet brought into reconciling and transforming relationship with the risen Christ. But already, in God's ongoing relation with all things through continuous creation, all creatures are *in* God and God is present *in* all creatures, enabling them to be and to become. This position that I am advocating can be called a form of *panentheism* (all things in God), but because it holds that God wonderfully transcends creation, it is sharply distinguished from all forms of *pantheism* (all things are God).

The insight that God is Persons-in-Mutual-Relations suggests a worldview and a praxis in which relations are primary.[28] If the central religious message is that relations are primary, then this grounds our commitment to other humans as a commitment to equal and mutual relations. It also grounds our ecological commitment to other creatures. We understand ourselves as caught up with them in a relational world as fellow creatures before a relational God. We can imagine the God–world relation in terms of the universe coming to be within the ambit of the divine relations. Evolution takes place within God.

3 The God of Evolution as a God of Free Self-Limitation in Love

IN CHAPTER 2, I PROPOSED that the God who creates through evolution is to be understood as Persons-in-Mutual-Relations, that this God creates an interrelated world, and that the unfolding of creation can be thought of as taking place within the divine relations of mutual love. I have suggested that this relational approach to the theology of God provides the basic foundation for an evolutionary theology.

But there is more that must be said. A theological approach to evolution must come to terms with the costs of evolution. The evolution of life is exuberant, bountiful, and beautiful. It is awe-inspiring. But it can also strike the human observer as destructive and alien. There are aspects of the evolution of life that human beings can find unpleasant, disturbing, and frightening. These include the evolutionary dead ends and mass extinctions of uncounted species, as well as the predation, pain, and death that are a constant part of the process.

This negative side of evolution, associated with the struggle for survival, can lead observers to see nature as cruel or capricious. For those who believe that God is the author of creation through evolutionary process, the evolutionary competition for life raises a fundamental question about God: Is the God who creates in such a way cruel and capricious?

Creation as Divine Self-Limitation

I suggest that the most important response to the negative side of evolution is found in a theology of a self-limiting
God.[1] But before pursuing this line of thought, I mention
briefly three points that I think are worth keeping in mind in
any approach to nature's "cruelty." First, in any authenti-
cally *theological* approach to natural evil, we must stand with
the Book of Job (38–42) before the mystery of God and God's
creation, and acknowledge that there is a great deal we do
not know. We do not know, for example, what the experience of nonhuman creatures is like. We know what suffering
is for human beings, but we have no way of knowing to
what extent a creature without language suffers in the way
that a self-conscious human being does. We commonly (and
properly, in my view) make an assumption that creatures
with developed brains and nervous systems suffer more
than others. But there is much we do not know about the
experience of nonhuman creatures. Daniel Dennett sees a
close evolutionary relation between nonhuman brains and
human consciousness. At the end of a recent book, however,
he points out how little we know about the minds of nonhuman animals:

> "It may not be able to talk, but surely it thinks!"—one of the
> main aims of this book has been to shake our confidence in
> this familiar reaction. Perhaps the biggest obstacle in our
> attempts to get clear about the mental competencies of non-
> human animals is our almost irresistible habit of imagining
> that they accompany their clever activities with a stream of
> reflective consciousness something like our own. It is not
> that we now know that they don't do any such thing; it is
> rather that in these early days of our investigations we must
> not assume that they do.[2]

Dennett certainly believes that *ethically*, in our interactions with other species, we must err on the side of caution, on the side of attribution of painful experience to other species. But he points out that pain and suffering are not the same thing, and that even with humans not all pain is experienced as suffering. Sometimes, for example, we dissociate ourselves from a painful experience. Humans, too, make a distinction between the pain of stubbing one's toe and what we normally mean by human suffering. Dennett puts forward the hypothesis that nonhuman animals experience pain but cannot suffer in the way humans can. But he suggests that this hypothesis needs careful scientific testing through observation of animal lives, to see if we can find in animals anything like what we humans know as suffering.[3]

This is simply an argument for caution in our assessment of what other creatures experience. In terms of evolutionary history, it seems to me that we are not in a position to judge, for example, whether, from its own perspective, it was good for an individual dinosaur to live, even though it ended up as food for another creature and as a member of an extinct species. I do not believe that we are in a position to say, as some writers do, that creatures like this dinosaur are "victims" of evolution.[4]

Much more radically, we must first acknowledge with the Book of Job that we do not know much about God's experience of all of this. We cannot read the mind of the Creator. We certainly do not know the outcome of God's work of creation and new creation. We cannot see the full picture. Because of our limited perspective and our limited information, we are not in a position to stand in judgment on God's morality in creating through natural selection.

Second, it is important to understand natural selection in a nonmythological and nonanthropomorphic way. At the

most fundamental level natural selection is simply the dif-
ferential reproductive success that is built into nature.
When a theologian, biologist, or anyone else describes natural selection as "selfish," or nature as "cruel," this is an
anthropomorphic way of speaking. Words that properly
apply to human moral behavior have been transferred to a
process of nature. This is not a scientific or a theological
way of talking. The process of natural selection is not to be
judged in anthropomorphic terms any more than is the
process of stellar nucleosynthesis or the Big Bang itself.
Theologically, all these processes are to be seen as dimensions of the way God creates through the unfolding of
potentialities and laws that are built into the material universe. John Haught has said:

> There is no more theological difficulty in the remorseless
> law of natural selection, which is said to be impersonal and
> blind, than in the laws of inertia, gravity or any other imper-
> sonal aspects of science. Gravity, like natural selection, has
> no regard for our inherent personal dignity either. It pulls
> towards earth the weak and powerful alike—at times in a
> deadly way. But very few thinkers have ever insisted that
> gravity is a serious argument against God's existence. Per-
> haps natural selection should be viewed no less leniently.[5]

If natural selection is approached in a nonanthropomorphic
way, then the problem of the goodness of God in the light of
evil and suffering (theodicy) is not more intense with
regard to natural selection than it is with regard to other
dimensions of existence, particularly death itself. It is death
and extreme suffering that remain the real issues for theodicy. The problem of evil is not specific to natural selection.
In fact, once death is accepted as essential to biological life,
natural selection can be understood as a positive process

whereby the negativity of death is subsumed, in some circumstances, into a process which leads to wonderfully creative new possibilities for life.

Third, it is of fundamental importance to point out that what Christians take as central to the non-negotiable data of revelation is the inclusive and compassionate God revealed in Jesus of Nazareth. This is the God revealed finally in the cross, the God who identifies with the pain of the world. A further datum of revelation is that this God is radically faithful. If God is consistent and faithful, then theological logic demands that the qualities found in God's action in Jesus are also operative in God's action in and through natural selection. This means that, in spite of the costs of the process, those who accept biblical revelation will hold that God can be trusted in the process of creating through natural selection. Those, like myself, who take this position will want to hold together the data from revelation, that God is radically compassionate, with the data from evolutionary science, that evolution has serious costs. They will seek a theology of God that can affirm the divine compassion for the world, and at the same time face honestly the negative side of evolution.

This leads to what I think is the most important theological response to the loss and suffering associated with natural selection and biological life and death. The response calls into question the popular and traditional view that there are no limits to what God can do, and replaces it with a theology of God's free self-limitation in love. If one's view of God is of a being who is *absolutely* omnipotent, unencumbered by any limits of any kind whatsoever, then it is difficult to reconcile such a God with the pain and death that accompanies natural selection and still affirm divine goodness.

39

From the perspective outlined in chapter 2, that of the God of mutual friendship, it can be argued that God is not to be understood as absolutely unlimited, but rather is to be seen as a God who freely accepts the limits of loving finite and created beings. If God is understood in relational terms, then this suggests that God is also understood in terms of the limitations that are freely accepted in loving relationships. I am conscious that the view of the God–world relation that I am proposing agrees in some respects with positions developed within Whiteheadian Process Theology, although it differs from much process theology because of the emphasis I place on the Trinity, divine transcendence, and divine freedom in creation.[6] The first area of agreement is in a commitment to a relational theology. The second is the insistence that this relational theology involves a real, two-sided, but differentiated relationship between God and creatures, a relationship in which God becomes vulnerable.[7]

If God acts in a relational way, then God will not coerce the response of the other, but will respect the freedom of the other. Those who freely choose to give themselves in love to another become vulnerable to the other and choose to accept the limits of loving. Love that operates by persuasion rather than coercion accepts some form of dependence on the freedom of the other. In human experience of love, those with the greatest capacity for love are those who are free and secure enough to make room for another within their own world, those who can live trustingly in some interdependence with the freedom of another. It is those who have to control others who cannot risk the vulnerability of authentic friendship. For this reason, theologians have begun to rethink the theological tradition of divine omnipotence. Walter Kasper, for example, points out that

40

for biblical faith, divine omnipotence is really the divine capacity for love beyond all human comprehension. This means that God's omnipotence can be understood as God's capacity to enter into love with all its costs. Kasper writes, "It requires omnipotence to be able to surrender oneself and give oneself away; and it requires omnipotence to be able to take oneself back in the giving and to preserve the independence and freedom of the recipient."[8] This kind of power, the capacity to give and receive love, is not what many people think of when they hear the words *omnipotent God*. They will often think of a God who can do *absolutely* anything—of power without limits of any kind. But this is not the God revealed to us in Jesus Christ. In Jesus crucified we find that divine power, which, as the resurrection assures us, is a real power to save and heal, can look like utter foolishness. Paul, apparently in the context of disputes at Corinth over the possession of wisdom, pointed to the wisdom of God which is revealed in the utter absurdity of the cross: "For Jews demand signs and Greeks desire wisdom, but we proclaim Christ crucified, a stumbling block to Jews and foolishness to Gentiles, but to those who are called, both Jews and Greeks, Christ the power of God and the wisdom of God" (1 Cor 1:22–24). Divine power and divine wisdom are revealed in the cross of Jesus. If Christ crucified shapes our picture of divine power, then it becomes clear that what is at stake here is the divine capacity for vulnerable loving. The divine power revealed in the cross is not the absolute power of coercion, which can force reality to obey one's own whims or even one's legitimate desires. Omnipotence, understood in the light of the cross, is the supreme power to freely give one's self in love.

In the light of this, the divine act of creation can be understood as an act of love, by which the trinitarian Persons

41

freely make space for creation and freely accept the limits of the process. God relates to creatures and in the relating becomes vulnerable. God respects the integrity of nature, its processes, and its laws. And in creating and relating with human creatures, God freely accepts the vulnerability of personal love and enters into love with a divine capacity for self-giving love.

This concept of a God who freely accepts the limits of loving amounts to a significant development of the tradition on divine power that is found in mainstream patristic and medieval theology. However, in patristic and medieval theology, the omnipotent God could never act in a way that is contrary to the divine nature, which was always understood as love. And alongside the mainstream tradition there has always been a biblical theology of the divine dispossession and self-emptying (the *kenosis* of Philippians 2:7) in the incarnation and the cross. This biblical teaching has given rise to a number of kenotic theologies, which have had an important role in pointing to the way in which God can be thought of as suffering with a suffering world. In my view, this kind of kenotic theology plays an indispensable role in dealing not only with the issue of human suffering, but also with the issue of natural processes, including natural selection.

But it is essential that this theology of the divine kenosis be kept in balance with a theology of God's desire and *power* to bring healing and salvation. Kenotic theology must also be a theology of liberation. The biblical God is not impotent, but is, rather, powerful in love. And, as I argued in chapter 2, central as kenotic love is to the Christian understanding of divine love, it needs to be understood within the larger framework of trinitarian love of mutual friendship.

In a recent example of a kenotic theology, Lucien Richard has expressed what I am attempting to say here about God's self-limitation in creation:

> Creation involves a costly process. Creation is an act of kenotic love; in creating, God limits self and allows a cosmos to emerge with its own autonomy. God, in God's creative causality, makes room for human freedom and autonomy to emerge and for a natural order to be characterized by open-endedness and flexibility.... The God revealed in the self-limitation that is the incarnation is the same God who creates. Creation demands on the part of the Creator the same kenosis the incarnation demanded. Creation demands as much self-sacrifice as building the Body of Christ. The Creator has to work from inside creation, suffering its pains of growth and chancy development.[9]

It has long been recognized that God accepts the limitations of human freedom. Christians have always believed that God wants human beings to respond to the divine offer of love, but that God nevertheless respects the freedom of human beings to accept or reject this offer. It has always been clear, too, that sinful human freedom is the cause of massive suffering through violence and greed. In contemporary theology, alongside this view of God's respect for human freedom, there is a new emphasis on God's respect for the processes of nature. Richard and other theologians are rightly insisting that we need to think of God respecting and making room "for a natural order characterized by open-endedness and flexibility." A God who respects human freedom is vulnerable to the misuse of that freedom, and a God who respects natural processes is vulnerable to the limits of those processes.

John Polkinghorne has promoted this line of thought. He

points out that God's love and faithfulness apply not only to human beings but also to the physical universe. He sees God as giving a measure of freedom to all creation.[10] He sees God as the great *allower* and *respecter* of freedom, including the freedom of physical processes. Polkinghorne reminds us that theologians have long responded to the problem of evil by appealing to God's respect for human freedom, and to this traditional "free-will defense," he suggests adding what he calls the "free-process defense." If God is faithful, then God is committed not just to respect human freedom but to respect the integrity of the created universe, along with its laws and processes.

All of this means that God may *not* be free to overrule natural process. A God who creates through physical process may well be committed to the integrity of the process. If this is the case, then God is not free or able to simply abolish all suffering. God, in creating, accepts the limits of physical processes and of human freedom. The theology of incarnation and the theology of the cross point to a God of unthinkable vulnerability and self-limitation. It is this concept of God, I believe, which needs to be brought into relation with natural selection. If God is to be understood as consistent and faithful, then theological logic demands that the boundlessly compassionate God revealed in Jesus Christ is the same God who acts to create through evolutionary process. The God of natural selection is the liberating, healing, and inclusive God of Jesus.

Such a God will be understood as a God who freely accepts the limits of the process of emergence, a God who creates through the losses and gains of evolutionary history. It suggests a God engaged with creation, a God who respects the process, and a God who suffers with and delights in the unfolding of creation.

44

A God Who Creates Through the
Interplay of Chance and Lawfulness

The fossil record shows that life has not evolved in a simple upward sequence. As Stephen Jay Gould has said, evolution is more like a copiously branching bush than a straight line.[11] Many forms of life have ended up in extinction. Gould insists that progress does not define the history of life. Most of life has shown no evidence of movement toward increased complexity.[12] Life on Earth is still dominated by bacteria. Nevertheless, evolution has produced such marvels as orchids, lorikeets, kangaroos, and human beings. This has happened through the interplay of chance and lawfulness.

Random chance is an integral part of the evolutionary process. It appears that a good deal of evolutionary change occurs at the molecular level through random drift. And the genetic mutations that are the source of novelty in natural selection arise at random.[13] Some of these mutations are beneficial, but many are harmful. Without these random mutations, evolution through natural selection could not occur, because there would be no variation that could be passed on to another generation. But although evolution is entirely dependent on random mutation, evolution itself is not random. Evolution can be wonderfully creative because there is a process, natural selection, which tends to preserve what is useful for adaptation to an environment and to eliminate what is not useful.

It is mutation and natural selection working together that produce something as beautiful as a blue wren, and something as complex as the human brain. It is chance and lawfulness, randomness and order, interlocked in collaboration, that have brought forth the exuberant diversity of

45

life on Earth. It is chance operating within the framework of natural laws that accounts for the inherent creativity of nature. Random mutation and natural selection enable an exploration of the potential that is present in the laws and constraints of nature.

How does this understanding of the role of chance in evolution relate to the Christian view of God as the Creator? Jacques Monod, in his *Chance and Necessity*, argued that since evolution is grounded in "pure chance," there is no longer any point in talk of purpose or meaning in the universe.[14] This amounted to a powerful attack on the Christian view of God as Creator, an attack that has been carried on in a different form in recent years by writers on evolution like the biologist Richard Dawkins and the philosopher Daniel Dennett.[15]

A number of eminent biologists insist that they find no evidence of purpose at work in evolution. Ernst Mayr has said that science has not found any teleological mechanisms that would justify us talking about overall purpose.[16] And, as I indicated earlier, Stephen Jay Gould denies that progress or increased complexity is characteristic of life as a whole. He argues that if we could play the tape of life again, the vast majority of replays would not produce a creature with self-consciousness. He claims that we human beings are "glorious accidents of an unpredictable process with no drive to complexity, not the expected results of evolutionary principles that yearn to produce a creature capable of understanding the mode of its own necessary construction."[17] If biologists like Mayr and Gould are right, they are right as biologists. They are saying that biology does not give empirical evidence of purpose at work in the universe. As a theologian, I would note, that supposing that they are right about the state of biological evidence, this does not rule out a theological principle of purpose. It is quite possible to think theologically of God as working purposefully in the universe through processes such as random mutation and natural selection, which when investigated empirically do not reveal purpose at all. Theologically, it is possible to think of God's purposes being achieved through what appears to empirical biology to be without purpose.[18]

The Darwinian view of evolution springing from variation and natural selection is not necessarily opposed to the idea of God as a purposeful Creator. It is certainly opposed to simplistic views of God creating through a series of divine interventions. But it is not in conflict with a view of God creating in and through natural processes, including chance and natural laws. Thomas Aquinas (1225–1274) long ago clarified that God's way of acting in the world (what can be called primary causality) is not opposed to the whole network of cause and effect in nature (secondary causality). God's work is achieved in and through creaturely cause and effect. It is not in competition with it. Aquinas never knew Darwin's theory of evolution, but he would have had no difficulty in understanding it as the way that God creates.

But first it is relevant to note that sciences such as physics and cosmology suggest that there is some direction in the emergence of the known universe.[19] These sciences tell us that the universe unfolded over the last ten to twenty billion years from the Big Bang. They describe the emergence of hydrogen and helium in the early universe, the formation of galaxies, the cooking of fundamental elements in the process of nucleosynthesis in stars, the formation of more complex elements and the "seeding" of the universe with these elements in supernova explosions, the emergence of our solar system around a second- or third-generation star, and the cooling of our own planet to a condition in which life could emerge.

Cosmologists point out that remarkably small changes in the fundamental characteristics of matter would have the result that life and conscious human beings could never have existed. The universe has to be remarkably "fine-tuned" to be the kind of universe in which human beings could emerge. Some have taken the view that the initial conditions of the universe and fundamental laws of physics are "fine-tuned" the way they are *in order that* something like the human mind might emerge. This is called the "Strong Anthropic Principle."[20] It is rejected by most scientists for lack of evidence. In its weaker form (the "Weak Anthropic Principle"), the theory simply points out what scientists take to be obvious, that the universe is in fact able to produce human beings, and if it were different, human beings would not be here to observe it. Scientists point out that, for example, the universe needs to be as old as it is and as big as it is, if all the processes necessary for the emergence of life on Earth are to take place. The carbon that is so important for our bodies, for example, could not exist if the carbon atoms had not been formed in the intense heat of stars. The stars could never have lit up if galaxies had not formed. Galaxies could never have formed if there was not just the right balance between the rate of expansion of the universe, the force of gravity, and the total mass of the universe. If, for example, gravity had been only a tiny fraction weaker, the power of expansion would have taken over, and there would be no galaxies, stars, or human beings. An "exquisite sensitivity" is needed in the fine-tuning of initial conditions and the characteristics of matter at the beginning of the universe if a universe that is hospitable to life is to emerge.

This fine-tuning of the universe is part of the story that contemporary science tells, as is the emergence of life through biological evolution. The story of the universe provides the context within which evolution occurs. It also suggests that there is more directionality in the process than some biologists have allowed. Writers like Gould have insisted that evolution is not to be thought of as a movement that has a clear direction or line. But while this does justice to some dimensions of evolution, it is not the whole story. Alongside all the forms of life that did not move toward increased complexity, there is also a story of development, which runs from the single-cell bacteria to the human mind and human culture. And this story is part of a larger story of the emergence of a universe which in fact is fine-tuned in such a way that life and eventually human beings can emerge within it.

For the theologian, this story of the universe, as it is told by contemporary sciences, can be understood as the way in which God creates. God creates a universe with initial conditions and physical constants which are fine-tuned so that life and consciousness might emerge. Long before life made its first appearance, the universe was already set on a course in which life and consciousness could evolve. The Creator is understood as influencing the process not only through its laws and initial conditions, but also through engagement with the process at every point in the relationship. It is this continual creation which enables the universe to exist and to unfold. It is this ongoing creative activity of God that enables life to emerge and to evolve through the process of natural selection.

One must acknowledge that thinking of God creating through genetic mutation and natural selection involves a significant shift in the way we image God. God is now pictured as involved creatively in an open-ended process that involves both randomness and lawfulness. It may well be that this kind of process is the best way to create a universe. It is certainly the way to create the kind of universe we have—open-ended process and randomness are intrinsic to the universe we inhabit. D. J. Bartholomew has urged that chance "plays a constructive role in creating a richer environment than would otherwise be possible." He sees chance as giving the Creator advantages that it is difficult to envisage being obtained in any other ways. He believes that there is every reason to think that a Creator who wished to achieve certain ends, such as intelligent creatures, might choose to reach those ends by means of random but creative processes.[21]

The theologian Edward Farley points out that random mutation is actually a condition for life in an environment that is subject to change:

> Evolution is the very condition of life as we know it. If DNA were utterly invariable, perfectly replicating every trait, nothing would have developed out of the primeval algal matter. Further, even if an existing species was created all at once by a divine magician, but utterly without cell mutations, it would not have a variable enough gene pool for its individuals to be able to adapt to changing conditions. Such a species, doomed to exactly repeat itself and unable to adapt, would succumb to the first environmental change. Hence the randomness of cell mutation is a sine qua non for the origin and continuation of any and every species. Evolution then is the necessary condition of organic life in a changing environment.[22]

In the world as we know it, biological life is inconceivable apart from evolution through random mutation.

Arthur Peacocke argues that we need to conceive of God as "involved in explorations of the many kind of unfulfilled potentialities of the universe," potentialities which have been given to the universe by God. According to Peacocke, there are propensities in nature which God has "built in." These "load the dice" in favor of life, increased complexity, and consciousness. Like Bartholomew, he sees the role of chance as "simply what is required if all the potentialities of the universe, especially for life are to be elicited effectively."[23] Peacocke sees God as an explorer in creation. He expresses this insight with a beautiful image taken from musical composition— God is like a composer able to unfold all the hidden possibilities of a theme. Thus God can be imagined as enabling the unfolding of the potentialities of the universe, potentialities which God has given to it, nurturing through divine redemptive and providential actions those that are to come to fruition in the community of free beings. Peacocke understands God as the "Improviser of unsurpassed ingenuity." God at work in creation is like Johann Sebastian Bach composing a complex and beautiful fugue, or better still, *improvising* on a theme at the keyboard. He notes that introducing improvisation into this image of God as composer "incorporates that element of open adaptability which any model of God's relation to a partly non-deterministic world should, however inadequately, represent."[24]

In a recent work, Keith Ward points out, rightly in my view, that God's creative action must be understood as universal in time and space, as a constantly influencing factor, which does not interrupt or interfere with the proper powers of finite causes, but cooperates with them:

One may think of God as having a universe-long intention to bring conscious beings into a community of freely chosen loving relationships. This intention will shape the initial laws of the universe and the emergence of more complex possibilities within it. In general, God will exert the maximum influence for good compatible with the preservation of the relative autonomy of nature and its probabilistic laws, and with the freedom of finite agents. God's causality will be physically undetectable, since the divine influence is not a quantifiable property, like mass or energy. But it will be an ultimate parameter or constraint, which affects every part of the physical universe in a different way, depending on the context and organized complexity of each part.[25]

Ward is right to insist that divine action is "physically undetectable." What we detect are, by definition, the interrelated causes and effects of creaturely existence. I differ from him when he argues that "natural selection is a necessary but not a sufficient condition for emergent evolution" and seems to suggest that God is needed as an explanation alongside natural selection.[26] I would want to argue that God is not to be understood as another factor operating alongside natural selection, or in addition to it, but is rather to be understood as acting through it.

I believe that God's purposes can best be understood as being achieved not in spite of, but *in and through* the indeterminacy that is built into the process of natural selection. I believe that we must hold together God's capacity to achieve God's purposes and the integrity of the process of evolution. The apparent paradox must be acknowledged. The *unpredictability* that seems to lie at the heart of the process of genetic mutation does not, at first glance, seem to be the way God could achieve divine *purposes*. But it is important to recall the theological principle that tells us that when we use words like *achieving purposes* and *action* of God, we are using analogies taken from the human experience of purposeful action. Does not the doctrine of divine transcendence suggest that God might achieve purposes in a way that radically transcends all human notions of achieving purposes? Once this transcendence of "divine action" is acknowledged, then it is reasonable to think of divine purposes being achieved through a process, random mutation, which in scientific terms is understood as chance-filled and purposeless.

The reason I argue that this position should be held is that it respects both the datum of biological evolutionary science (the randomness of mutations) and the datum of theology (the purposefulness of divine action). The alternative is to undermine the best insights of evolutionary science (as some religious thinkers do) or to undermine the theological claim regarding divine purposes (as some scientifically trained thinkers do).

This position does not bring divine purposeful action and the unpredictable process of evolution into a completely satisfying synthesis. What it affirms, on the basis of the transcendence of divine action, is that God can work creatively, adventurously, and purposefully in and through processes that are unpredictable. It affirms that God can be thought of as working purposefully in and through the chance and lawfulness of biological evolution. Once the real transcendence of God is acknowledged, then the transcendence of divine "action" can and must be acknowledged.

The theological tradition holds that God can be at work creatively and purposefully in and through human actions that are yet completely free. In fact Karl Rahner has put forward as a fundamental axiom of theology that human freedom and dependence on God grow in equal not inverse proportions.[27] The intuitive or common sense approach would be that the more we are dependent on God the less free we are. Rahner insists that the more we grow in authentic freedom the more we are dependent on God and in authentic union with God. God's purposes are accomplished through the contingency of human freedom. In a similar way, I believe, God can work artfully and purposefully in the unpredictability and contingency of nature—the "freedom" of nature.

John Haught points out that if we think of God as operating in a persuasive rather than a coercive manner, then we might expect an aspect of indeterminacy or randomness in nature. We would expect God to want nature to have a degree of "freedom" of autonomy. He suggests that if God were to create like a magician with total control of things, then the result would be an impoverished world, lacking the drama, diversity, adventure, and beauty that evolution has produced. He asks: "But might it not be because God wants the world and beings within the world to partake of the divine joy of creating novelty that the cosmos is left unfinished, and that it is invited to be at least to some degree self-creative?"[28] He argues that behind the process of natural selection, there is something "silently, persuasively, and unobtrusively operative in promoting the over-all cosmic movement from simplicity to complexity." He finds what he calls an "extravagant Generosity" underlying the whole cosmic process.[29] This divine generosity allows the universe its own autonomy and its own role in contributing to the unfolding of creation.

The Creator that Arthur Peacocke describes as the "Improviser of unsurpassed ingenuity" and that John Haught calls "extravagant Generosity" can also be imaged in other ways. The God who creates through natural selection, and the interplay of chance and lawfulness, might be thought of as a painter at work on a canvas, as a writer with a poem coming to birth within his or her consciousness, as a gardener developing a beautiful landscape, as a host preparing a meal for friends. Two insights are important in all these images: first, the work is exploratory and improvising; second, the artist can only work with what is there, with the possibilities and constraints offered by the materials and the subjects of the work. What is original and beautiful comes from the interplay of creativity and respect for what is already there.

4 · *Human Beings Before God in an Evolutionary World*

T HE FOCUS OF THIS BOOK is on the doctrine of *God* in the light of evolutionary biology. But the theology of God cannot be separated from God in relationship to *us*—from theological anthropology. This immediately opens up the areas of grace and original sin, traditionally key areas of interest in theological anthropology. How are original sin and grace understood in a theology that takes evolution seriously? In this chapter, I first offer a brief account of the scientific understanding of human prehistory. Then I describe some recent approaches to a theology of original sin in the light of evolution, and follow this by offering my own suggestions on this complex issue. In a fourth section I consider briefly the theology of grace. Finally, I discuss the creation of the spiritual dimension of the human person.

Human Evolution

Richard Leakey, in a recent book on the origin of humankind, points out that while there is no agreement among scientists about the detail of human prehistory, there is, nonetheless, a great deal of agreement about its broad outline.[1] He identifies four key stages in this outline of the emergence of human beings.

The first stage occurred about seven million years ago in Africa, with the evolution of an apelike species that had an upright *(bipedal)* style of walking. This was a major biological innovation, involving a differently shaped pelvis, with significant changes in bone structure, the arrangement of muscles, and the movement of limbs. It seems likely that these first bipedal creatures were humanlike only in their way of moving. In all other ways (such as in the food they ate and in the shape of their skulls, jaws, and teeth) they would have resembled apes. But the adoption of bipedalism was loaded with evolutionary potential—it enabled the upper limbs to be free and would make it possible for descendants of these creatures to manipulate tools. The second stage of human prehistory is the proliferation of bipedal species between five million and two million years ago. Various hominid species evolved in a process that biologists call "adaptive radiation." Anthropologists, in referring to the hominids of this period, commonly describe a more graceful group called *Australopithecus africanus* (which means "southern ape from Africa") and a more robust group called *Australopithecus robustus.*

In the third stage, between three and two million years ago, one group developed a significantly larger brain. The increase in brain size appears in *Homo habilis,* the first creatures to be classified under the genus *Homo.* In this period, then, two types of bipedal creatures existed side by side: one type had a small brain and large cheek teeth (the various *australopithecine* species); the other type had a larger brain and smaller teeth *(Homo).* The *australopithecine* species all died out by about a million years ago, while a number of species of *Homo* survived. *Homo erectus* seems to have emerged about two million years ago. *Homo erectus* was the first hominid to use fire, the first to run like modern humans, the first to hunt consistently, the first to make stone tools according to plan, and the first to range beyond Africa. *Homo erectus* had a larger brain and a more athletic body than other species. To what extent was *Homo erectus* a communicating self-conscious creature like modern human beings? Leakey writes:

> We don't know definitively whether *Homo erectus* possessed a degree of spoken language, but several lines of evidence suggest this. And we don't know, and probably never will know whether this species experienced a degree of self-awareness, a humanlike consciousness, but my guess is that it did. Needless to say, language and consciousness, which are among the most prized features of *Homo sapiens*, leave no trace in the prehistoric record.[2]

The fourth stage is marked by the appearance of *modern humans (Homo sapiens)*—creatures fully equipped with language, consciousness, artistic imagination, and the capacity for advanced technological innovation. There is a vigorous debate among scientists about the emergence of modern humankind. Part of the background to the emergence of modern humans is the existence of other human species in Europe, Asia, and Africa in the period between half a million and 34,000 years ago. The various other varieties of *Homo* of this period are sometimes called "archaic *sapiens*." They have a larger brain than *Homo erectus*, but compared to *Homo sapiens*, they are thick-skulled and robustly built.[3] There is a great deal of evidence about one of these groups, the Neanderthals, who lived between about 135,000 and 34,000 years ago, inhabiting an area from Western Europe to Asia.

What is the relationship between Neanderthals and modern humans? One approach to the evolution of modern humans is the "multiregional hypothesis." In this view, *Homo erectus* expanded out of Africa nearly two million years ago. Evolution toward modern humans then occurred in the different regions inhabited by *Homo erectus*. In Europe, for example, *Homo erectus* evolved into Neanderthals, who then

evolved into modern humans. In this theory, genetic conti-
nuity was maintained by means of interbreeding and gene
flow between the various populations. This ensured that
these scattered populations moved toward the same evolutionary outcome—*Homo sapiens*.[4]

The alternative and more recent approach is the "Out of
Africa" hypothesis advocated by Chris Stringer and others.
In this view, modern *Homo sapiens* evolved only very
recently in Africa and from there spread quickly to Asia and
Europe, eventually replacing existing populations such as
the Neanderthals. In this view, Neanderthals are not the
ancestors of modern humans but more like our evolutionary cousins. Chris Stringer and Robin McKie offer a tentative timetable:

> It all seems to paint a fairly fragmentary but nonetheless
> cogent picture of our exodus from Africa, one that suggests
> a fundamental timetable for our colonisation of the world.
> Firstly, we moved from Africa to Asia about 100,000 years
> ago and spread eastward until we reached New Guinea and
> Australia by about 50,000 years ago. A little later, having
> conquered the east, mankind also dispersed westward from
> Asia and drifted into Europe, eventually extinguishing
> Neanderthals there. Finally, at some point, Asian people
> made their way over Beringia and speedily down through
> the Americas, their progress unencumbered by the presence
> of other hominid competitors.[5]

By 30,000 years ago, modern humans were the only human
species left on Earth. Stringer and McKie suggest that they
may have had a breeding population of about 300,000.

The debate between the multiregional-evolution and the
Out of Africa hypotheses continues. Despite having some
sympathy for the multiregional approach, Richard Leakey

offers cautious support for the Out of Africa hypothesis.[6] He points out that a majority of population geneticists support this view. Theology can only wait for the detailed picture to be clarified by ongoing scientific work.

In the meantime, it is the task of theology to dialogue with the broad approach to human origins that is supported at present by the mainstream of science: that human beings had their origins in Africa between five and seven million years ago, with the advent of bipedalism; that over the next few million years various species of bipedal apes (*Australopithecus*) evolved; that two to three million years ago, there was a major increase of brain size, with the evolution of *Homo habilis*, soon followed by *Homo erectus*, who spread from Africa to other parts of the old world; that modern humans evolved from *Homo erectus* either in various regions or, according to the more recent theory, in Africa about 200,000 years ago, spreading from there to Asia and Europe about 100,000 years ago.[7]

Original Sin and Evolution: Recent Theologies

How can original sin be understood in the light of this story of human evolution? In attempting to offer some response to this question, I survey three recent theologies that relate original sin to biological evolution. I concentrate on the third of them, that of Philip Hefner, since he has brought much of the discussion together in his synthesis.[8]

First, Charles Birch and John Cobb, following Reinhold Niebuhr, recognize that there is a tension between our biological natures and human culture, but refuse to locate sin in either nature or culture. With Niebuhr, they insist that sin springs from the human will.[9] In this sense the "fall" is part of human existence and human experience everywhere.

60

But Birch and Cobb also suggest a connection between the symbol of the fall and biological evolution. The fall can be thought of as an evolutionary "fall upward." For each evolutionary step there is a cost—an experience of the fall. In this sense, the fall "identifies the occurrence of a new level of order and freedom bought at the price of suffering."[10] Animal life, human life, cultural evolution, Neolithic culture, urban civilization, the industrial revolution may all have opened up new possibilities and brought new freedoms. But each liberation brings new sufferings and new possibilities of enslavement.

Gabriel Daly also sees the fall in terms of the movement from one level of evolution to another. He understands it as an alienation from peace at one level in order to attain it at a higher level. He points out that this has particular relevance for the human creature, which has had to embark on a phase of evolution that is cultural, rather than simply biological. In this movement, human beings necessarily bring their biological past with them. They go forward "weighed down by a genetically produced nostalgia" for their animal past. Daly sees this nostalgia as locked into our bones and flowing in our veins.[11] The appetites, instincts, drives, and energies that bring satisfaction to other animals are not enough to bring peace to the self-aware human creature, but they remain in the human being alongside the newly developed awareness of right and wrong. The old instincts can reassert themselves at any point—as in the case of a hit-and-run driver whose instinct is to get away from a threatening situation. Does this suggest that these instincts and drives that are proper to nonhuman primates become sin when they are found in human beings? Daly's response is that they are not sin, since they come from the hands of the Creator, but they can become the instruments of sin if they

61

are not shaped and healed by grace.[12] There are a host of primal emotions within us (aggression, jealousy, possessive love, fear) that can destroy us and our relationships if we do not name them and come to terms with them. These are what the classical doctrine of original sin has called the "tinder of sin" *(fomes peccati)*, but, Daly insists, they are also the "raw material of holiness."[13]

Daly points to the Jungian insight that there is a price to pay when human beings distance themselves from their instincts through repression. Failure to face the demands of the unconscious can result in mental and emotional disturbance and in an obstruction to wholeness. Daly sees a loss of innocence in the evolutionary advance to self-consciousness. Cultural evolution gives rise to the gratuitous infliction of hurt by human individuals and groups on other humans and upon the natural environment. Sin finds expression in human cultural evolution. We have a fallen history, but our history is also a history of grace and salvation. These two dimensions of human cultural history are symbolized for Daly in two institutions, the concentration camp and the hospital.

Philip Hefner offers two lines of thought on a theology of original sin in the light of evolution. His first suggestion is that original sin can be understood in terms of *discrepancy* between the information coming to us from our genetic inheritance and from our culture. He sees *Homo sapiens* as a creature dependent upon and formed by two kinds of information, genetic and cultural. Genes and culture have come together in the human to form a symbiosis or supra-organism, which flourishes precisely because the two sources of information have coadapted both to each other and to the environment. Although the human person is a real unity, there is dissonance and tension between the two sources of information. Hefner argues that the concepts of the fall and original sin may be considered as "mythic renditions of this biologically grounded sense of discrepancy."[14] He sees this sense of discrepancy as deeply rooted in our being and as primordial in our self-awareness, and therefore as "original."

There are a number of aspects of this discrepancy which Hefner names. First, modern humans experience a *loss of the immediacy* that their ancestors had with their own nature and their environment. Second, some of the *information from our genetic past can appear ethically unacceptable* to us today (such as some expressions of the tendency to territoriality). Third, there is a sense of *finitude and guilt about our incapacity to satisfy our biologically given motivators* (such as the drive to excel).[15] Fourth, there is in us a *clash between cooperation and altruism* on the one hand and *our genetic selfishness* on the other. To illustrate this last point, Hefner refers to Donald Campbell's claim that urban living is made possible by culture, which acts against the genetic urge toward competition.[16] Campbell and Hefner both see this state of affairs as related to the doctrine of original sin.

Alongside this idea that original sin is related to discrepancy between information coming from genes and culture, Hefner makes a second contribution to the discussion on original sin. He points to human *fallibility,* which he says, shows that sinfulness is intrinsic to the human condition. Cultural evolution, like biological evolution, occurs only through the process of trial and error. But this process is accompanied by a consciousness of fallibility. Human freedom emerges in probing forward, but this movement forward is always connected with a sense of inadequacy and guilt. The fallibility that gives rise to error and evil is intrinsic to the human being and is basic to the process that gives rise to life and enables its enrichment. So, Hefner sees this process as good. But, in his view, this good process is always accompanied by failure and sin.[17]

Original Sin in Evolutionary Context: A Proposal

Hefner sees original sin first in terms of the *discrepancy* we experience between information coming from our genes and from our culture, and second in terms of the *fallibility* and limitation that are essential to human evolution.

In my view, Hefner's insights, along with those of Birch and Cobb, and Daly, genuinely illuminate the human condition. Great thinkers like Paul, Augustine, and Luther have described the existential struggle that characterizes human existence in the world, the gap between what we would do and what we do, the sheer weight that opposes our best intentions, our seeming inability to give ourselves completely, our incapacity to love with our whole hearts. Our appetites and passions erupt in unruly disorder, our wills seem fettered, our minds cluttered and confused. This inner state of affairs has been called concupiscence in the theological tradition. It has generally been understood as the result of original sin, and Luther identified it as sin. What Hefner does is to help us understand this inner disorder in the light of our evolutionary history as creatures who are a symbiosis of genes and culture, and as fallible creatures who move forward only through trial and error. To my mind, this evolutionary insight does help us understand ourselves. It offers genuine insight into part of what the Christian tradition has called concupiscence.

But there is a critical question that I would put to Hefner's position: Granted that we do experience discrepancy between information coming from genes and culture and that we experience ourselves as intrinsically fallible, are these experiences to be equated with sin? I argue that they are not. In attempting to move toward a new formulation on original sin in the light of evolution, I offer some reflections in the form of three theses.

Thesis 1: *Human beings are a fallible symbiosis of genes and culture, who experience drives and impulses from the genetic side of their inheritance as well as from the cultural side, and these drives and impulses can be disordered and mutually opposed. This experience is **intrinsic** to being an evolutionary human but it is **not** sin.*

As I have noted, the theological tradition has described the disordered drives and impulses that we experience as "concupiscence," and this concupiscence has been seen as the result of original sin. But Karl Rahner has offered a major clarification of the concept of concupiscence, one that has relevance in reflecting on our evolutionary inheritance.[18] He distinguishes between the disorder that springs from *sin* and the disorder that is intrinsic to being a *limited* and *finite* human being. Disorder of the first kind comes from the history of the sinful rejection of God, which partially shapes us and which is the context for our free decisions. But, Rahner insists, this *sinful* disorder must be distinguished from the second kind of disorder which is not the result of sin but which is intrinsic to being a spiritual creature who is at the same time radically *bodily* and *limited*. Because of our bodiliness and finitude, we human beings are never fully autonomous, integrated, or in control. Rahner, however, sees this is not as something to be overcome, but as part of God's good creation. This form of concupiscence is not sinful but morally neutral. Our bodies

65

can resist our wills not only when we make a good choice but also when we make a bad one. An example of our bodies resisting a bad choice is the experience we human beings have when a blushing face betrays a lie.

In the words of Stephen Duffy, we need to distinguish between the one form of concupiscence that is "the child of sin" and another that is simply "the companion of finitude."[19] Hefner points to the disorder in us that is there simply because we are finite evolutionary creatures. The discrepancy between genes and culture, the biologically inherited drives and instinctive reactions, the fallibility that is part of evolutionary history—all of these are the companion of finitude. This is not original sin, nor is it the concupiscence that springs from sin. It is simply part of being a finite human creature. We are evolutionary creatures who are intrinsically fallible. This is the way that God has created us. As Gabriel Daly has said, these kinds of disorders are not sin, but the "raw materials of holiness."

Thesis 2: *Original sin consists of the fact that human beings have a cultural history of personal and communal sin which enters into and becomes an inner dimension of each person's situation.*

We are not only evolutionary creatures who are fallible and limited, but also *children of sin* because the fallible symbiosis that is the human has rejected the Creator. Original sin has to do with the triune God. It has to do with the human stance before the God who is the source of genetic inheritance, and who in grace calls us into a life centered on love.

Original sin involves the inner effect on a person of the history of the human community's rejection of God and of their creaturely status before God. It is not the structure of the human (as a fallible symbiosis of genes and culture) that constitutes original sin, but the inner impact on each human person's free situation of previous human rejection of God. As Karl Rahner has pointed out, original sin has to do with the fact that we actualize ourselves as free subjects in a situation that is always determined by other persons and by history.[20] The sin of others is intrinsic to and partly constitutive of the situation of our human freedom. The sin of others is a universal and permanent part of the human condition from the beginning and is in this sense original.

This determination of our inner situation by the sin of others is called "sin" only in a loose and analogous sense. Strictly speaking, sin is personal and actual; it is the free and deliberate rejection of God. It is only for this kind of personal sin that we are morally responsible. Original sin means that the history of personal and communal sin enters into and becomes an inner dimension of each person's situation, but this is not yet our own personal sin. We are still free to choose between love and hate, between sin and grace. By way of an aside, it is important to note that if original sin is understood as springing from the history of human free decisions against God and God's creation, then nonhuman nature is not "fallen," except insofar as nature is damaged by human sin.[21] The ecological crisis makes it all too apparent that nature is damaged by human decisions. But the fundamental Christian insight about creation is not that creation is "fallen," but that all of creation will be transformed in Christ (Rom 8:18–25; Col 1:15–20).

Our existential state then is constituted by (1) our evolutionary structure as a fallible symbiosis of genes and culture, and (2) the additional fact that the history of human sin is an inner constitutive element in our own free acts. This second element twists, compounds, and distorts the complexity and fallibility that is part of our evolutionary makeup. It is only this second element that is properly associated with original sin.

Thesis 3: *Original sin has an impact on the whole person. It is **not** to be associated with only the biological side of the human; nor is it to be associated only with the cultural side. It involves our free response to both our genetic inheritance and our cultural conditioning.*

I believe that it is a mistake to identify selfishness and sin with the biological side of the human being. I think it is also a mistake to identify unselfish behavior with the cultural side. On the one hand, our genetic inheritance carries messages that are necessary for human life, and these are to be seen, according to biblical tradition, as part of God's good creation. On the other hand, culture, and religion as part of culture, can carry not only messages of altruistic love, but also messages of systemic evil. As I mentioned previously, Birch and Cobb rightly warn against the idea that we can pinpoint the source of moral evil either in nature or in human culture. They point out that it must be located in the responsible human being who sins against God.

Original sin, as the impact of accumulated history of sinful rejection of God, which enters into the inner place of our freedom, may involve a lack of acceptance and integration of either side of our humanity before God. When the biological side dominates, it is possible that powerful self-serving urges from our genetic side can obscure relational tendencies coming from the cultural inheritance. But at other times particular forms of cultural conditioning can so predominate that healthy genetic drives and life-giving impulses may be obscured or driven underground. Rejection of God may involve the distortion, denial, repression from consciousness, or the lack of integration of either side of our heritage. Both forms of denial can twist and distort the human before God.

It is essential to recall that culture can carry not only altruistic information, but also messages that legitimate the dominance of the powerful. Cultural messages can support the oppression of women, legitimate the exploitation of those who are poor and vulnerable in a society, and contribute to the marginalization of those who appear as "other." As Langdon Gilkey has said:

> Culture is the locus of the social institutions that pass on systemic injustice; it was culture's information system that perpetuated and justified slavery, and also class, gender, and racial domination. Culture is also the locus of the mores and morals that encourage, defend and justify those unjust (and cruel) institutions. Culture is the site of ideology, whether religious or secular, which incites, increases, and excuses, in fact justifies through its myths and rituals, these injustices.[22]

There are instances where it seems apparent that genes and culture together are involved in structural sin, which is sin carried in culture. Patriarchal culture, for example, with its support for the position of dominant males and for structures of oppressive power over others, is obviously sin carried in culture. But this form of cultural sin may build, at least in some part, on genetic tendencies inherent in the sexual relations of our prehuman ancestors. Extreme militarism may be understood, in part, as a radically destructive culture, but it also seems that it may give expression to genetic urges we share with our prehuman ancestors about dominance and territoriality.

The intellectual and technological capacity of human culture greatly enlarges the genetic and cultural capacity in human beings to do damage to other creatures. Competition for survival and predation in nature involve the death of many creatures. But when competitive instincts are enfleshed in unintegrated, technologically powerful and sinful human beings, the capacity for death and destruction involves the whole planetary community. Self-serving genetic tendencies can be "amplified" by the enormous capacities of human culture and human technology. The self-serving actions of a chimp may have negative effects on a small number of other creatures, but the unintegrated self-serving human being, with all the power and resources of human culture, can destroy the rain forest of the Earth and drive the uncounted species that inhabit them to extinction.

Genetic and cultural inheritances are profoundly interrelated in human evolutionary development. They are so closely connected that we cannot properly attribute behavior patterns simply to one side of our inheritance. We cannot locate sin in our genetic inheritance. We are not genetically determined even though we may well be subject to genetic tendencies.[23] Original sin is not to be understood as springing from one side of the human, but rather from the history of human free decisions which enters into the inner place of our own decision making.

Grace in Evolutionary Context

It is not simply the history of sin that enters into the free situation of every person, but also the reality of God's grace. Paul tells us that "where sin increased, grace abounded all the more" (Rom 5:20). How is this ever-abounding grace to be understood in terms of our evolutionary history?

Contemporary theology and the teaching of the Second Vatican Council have made it abundantly clear that God's grace cannot be limited to the Christian church, but must be understood as having a universal outreach. Karl Rahner, for example, argues that all human beings everywhere and always exist as surrounded, shaped, and constituted by the presence of God's grace. He sees grace as the self-communication of God. Grace means that the trinitarian God is always freely and graciously present in self-offering love to every human person. God creates in order to give Godself in love. The triune God surrounds and embraces every human person in radical nearness, so that this divine self-offer is a constitutive dimension of human existence. According to Rahner, this self-offering love, which is always present, can be explicitly or implicitly rejected—as sin. It can also be explicitly or implicitly accepted in justifying faith. We live in a world of grace. Rahner's theology of grace is summed up in his saying that the human person is "the event of a free, unmerited and forgiving, and absolute self-communication of God."[24]

What this means in an evolutionary framework is that we can think of our ancient forbears coming to self-consciousness in a world that was already a world of grace. Of course it would also have been a world of danger and fear. Our ancestors must have come to consciousness in a world that was extremely threatening. Perhaps their rituals and myths can be seen both as a way of taming the terrors of life and as an attempt to give expression to the experience of a grace.

It seems to me that we can have no certain knowledge about exactly when this happened. It is linked to the emergence of self-awareness, and there is no agreement about this. Richard Leakey points out that prior to 100,000 years ago, there is no evidence of any kind of ritual or art that would betray reflective consciousness. The earliest evidence of deliberate burial is a Neanderthal burial that took place a little more than 100,000 years ago. Leakey sees Neanderthals and other archaic *sapiens* groups as having a highly developed reflective consciousness. He suggests, nevertheless, that their consciousness would not have been as luminous as our own. Our consciousness has benefited from the emergence of modern language. Modern language and modern consciousness have emerged together. What about the self-awareness of the ancient *Homo erectus?* Leakey says that he would find it surprising if late *Homo erectus* "did not have a level of consciousness significantly greater than that of chimpanzees." He says of *Homo erectus* that their "social complexity, large brain size, and probable language skills" all point to a developed level of consciousness.[25]

Clearly there is no way of pinpointing when our ancestors first came to experience reality as we do. As Leakey himself says, such a question may be unanswerable. What a theologian can suggest is that, whenever there was the first, perhaps childlike self-awareness, then this can be seen as the beginning of human experience of a world of grace. This grace, understood as God present in self-offering love, was already there. A gracious God was already there in the rise of bipedalism, already there in the first forms of life, and already there in the origin of the universe. The theological story of the emergence of human awareness is the story of emergence into a gracious universe.

The Theological Issue of the Spiritual Dimension of the Human

The scientific evidence for evolution has been accepted by many Christian churches, but not by fundamentalist Christians. In the Roman Catholic Church, for example, over the last fifty years there has been a cautious openness to evolution. There has also been development in the official teaching of this church about evolution. In 1950, Pope Pius XII wrote on evolution and Christian faith.[26] He presented evolution as a serious hypothesis, worthy of in-depth investigation, alongside opposing hypotheses. He warned that evolution should not be adopted as if it were a certain doctrine, and as if one could prescind completely from the teaching of revelation. But he taught that there was no necessary opposition between evolution and Christian faith. He pointed to the conditions on which this doctrine would be compatible with Christian faith. These included safeguarding the doctrine of original sin and the immediate creation of the spiritual soul by God.

In 1996, another pope, John Paul II, returned to these issues in a widely publicized address to the Pontifical Council of Sciences.[27] In this address, John Paul II concludes that new knowledge has led to the recognition that evolution is *more than a hypothesis.* This new evidence comes from a variety of independent sources: "It is indeed remarkable that this theory has been progressively accepted by researchers, following a series of discoveries in various fields of knowledge. The convergence, neither sought nor fabricated, of the results of work that was conducted independently is in itself a significant argument in favor of this theory."[28] This is a substantial advance on the position taken by Pius XII. John Paul II makes it clear that he can endorse a scientific methodology that, on the basis of empirical evidence, describes and measures the multiple manifestations of life and places them upon a time line. At the same time, he clearly holds and teaches the doctrine of original sin and the immediate creation of the human soul. He calls for a philosophical and theological exploration of evolution, which respects both the "ontological difference" that marks human beings as spiritual creatures and the "ultimate meaning of the Creator's designs."

The Harvard biologist, Stephen Jay Gould, responded to this address with an interesting and appreciative reflection on this movement in the official Roman Catholic position on the theory of evolution. He sees John Paul II as welcoming of the scientific evidence that has emerged over the last fifty years. In Gould's interpretation, the pope takes the stance: "It has been proven true; we always celebrate nature's factuality, and we look forward to interesting discussions of theological implications." Gould rejoices to find a church leader offering a positive approach to the issue of biological evolution. He describes it as good news and he recalls the wisdom saying: "As cold waters to a thirsty soul, so is good news from a far country" (Prv 25:25).[29]

Perhaps because he sees religion in ethical terms, Gould finds it appropriate for John Paul II, as a religious leader, to declare his ongoing commitment to the divine creation of the human soul and to comment on the ethical value of the human person. Gould declares himself to be personally skeptical about the soul, but he adds that he knows that "souls represent a subject outside the magisterium of science." His argument is that science and religion need not be in conflict because their teachings occupy different domains, and their *magisteria* (teaching authorities) are "nonoverlapping."[30]

The issue of God's creation of the spiritual dimension of the human being, in traditional language "the immediate creation of the soul by God," has been widely discussed in theology during the last fifty years. On the one hand, theologians have taught consistently that the emergence of the human species as self-conscious and spiritual beings, and the biological and spiritual life of each human being, occur through the action of the Creator God. On the other hand, they resist the interpretation of this divine action as an intervention. The concept of a particular divine *intervention* at the origin of the human species, or of a particular divine *intervention* for each individual person, does not seem satisfactory either scientifically or theologically. In terms of science, requiring individual divine interventions does not fit easily with what we know from science about evolutionary development. But more fundamentally, in terms of theology, it seems to reduce God to being a secondary cause alongside other secondary causes. The Creator tends to become understood as an interventionist God, constantly acting in creation alongside other causes.

Zoltan Alszeghi points out that the problem has been overcome by conceiving the divine action in the creation of the human, including all that makes up the spiritual dimension of humanity, as a creative action that "works through all the generations of living beings, so that everyone shares in this special but continuous action in the great work of universal evolution."[31] The creation of each human person as a spiritual being is understood as special and unique. Each human being is created in the divine image. But this occurs through God's *one continuous act of ongoing creation.*

Michael Schmaus, along with a great number of contemporary theologians, points out that the human being "is not a creature composed of two elements but is a single being in whom matter and spirit are essentially united."[32] He sees the spiritual dimension of human beings emerging from within the evolution of life, and springing from the material universe. But the human spirit is not simply an expression of matter and derived from matter. The emergence of self-conscious spiritual beings is something radically *new.* It needs explanation at the level of theology. It can be explained by the special action of the Creator, which is not to be understood in an interventionist sense, but as part of the process of divine ongoing creation by which God brings forth what is radically new from within the laws and constraints of nature.[33]

Karl Rahner also takes this line of thought. He explains the emergence of the human spirit in terms of his theology of "active self-transcendence." He sees the material universe as "oriented from within by God, in dynamic self-transcendence" toward the human person. In human beings, the world achieves "immanence, subjectivity, freedom, history and personal fulfilment." Rahner writes that in the human being, "the universe finds itself" and is "consciously confronted with its origin and goal." What Pius XII and others have spoken of as "immediate creation" of the human soul, Rahner tells us, can be understood as God making possible a self-transcendence of the material universe in the direction of the spiritual human person.[34]

What these theologians are suggesting is that God should not be thought of as creating individual human beings through a series of interventions, but as creating in one divine act that embraces the whole process. It is this one divine act that enables what is radically new to emerge in creation. Above all it enables the emergence of self-conscious and spiritual human beings. Each of them is created in radical uniqueness in the image of God. Each of them is invited into a unique interpersonal relationship with the triune God in the gift of grace. Each of them is destined for eternal life, which is a participation in the divine perichoretic life of friendship beyond comprehension. The creation of each spiritual being is individual, unique, and personal, but can be thought of as brought about through God's one divine action of continuous creation.

Human beings are part of the history of the universe. What is most particular to them is that they are part of the universe that has become self-conscious and is therefore able to enter into conscious relationship with the God who holds them in existence and invites them into communion. Are there other such creatures in the vastness of the universe? Theology, on its own resources, cannot answer this question. It must wait to see if science can offer any answers. What theology can affirm is that human beings are intimately connected with the whole universe in its evolutionary unfolding and that they have a capacity to relate to each other, to other creatures, and to God as creatures in whom the universe has come to self-conscious awareness.

5   *Evolution and the Holy Spirit*

THE THEME OF THIS BOOK is the relationship between biological evolution and the Christian theology of God as Trinity. This theme suggests a further important question: How are the *Persons* of the Trinity to be thought of in relation to evolution?

I believe that, in this context, there is not an urgent need for extended comment on the trinitarian Person who is usually named the Father, but who can also be thought of as the Mother who never forgets the children of her womb (Is 49:15). In relation to creation, this "first" Person of the Trinity has been always understood to be the "Source," "Fountain," and "Origin" from which all things spring. In solemn liturgical texts we direct our prayers to the one who is the "Source of life and goodness" (Eucharistic Prayer IV), and the "fountain of all holiness" (Eucharistic Prayer II). We use words such as these: "All life, all holiness come from you" (Eucharistic Prayer III) and "You have created all things to fill your creatures with every blessing" (Eucharistic Prayer IV). There is no doubt that Christians have always seen creation as springing ultimately from the one in the Trinity who is described by Bonaventure as the "Fountain Fullness" *(fontalis plenitudo)*. In some Christian circles this trinitarian Person is simply identified as "the Creator." While this is understandable, it runs the risk of seeming to suggest that there is no role in creation for the Word and the Spirit.

For the purposes of this book, I will assume that it is clear that this Fountain Fullness is the *ultimate Source* from which spring all the processes of creation, including the process of biological evolution. I will focus on the relationship of the Holy Spirit to creation, and to evolution in particular (the work of this chapter), and on the connection between the Word made flesh and biological evolution (the work of chapter 6).

How is the Holy Spirit related to the evolution of life? My search for an answer to this question begins with some insights on the Holy Spirit from Basil of Caesarea. Basil has an important place in the history of the doctrine of the Spirit. After the Council of Nicaea (325), debate about the divinity of the Word had continued and, in this context, the question of the status of the Holy Spirit became an issue for the Christian community. The divinity of the Spirit would not be explicitly articulated in a credal fashion until the First Council of Constantinople (381). This council took place after Basil's death (in 379 or perhaps 377), but Basil, in the period leading up to the council, was the major contributor to the doctrine of the Spirit, in collaboration with his friend Gregory Nazianzus and his brother Gregory of Nyssa.

In an early work, *Against Eunomius,* which appeared about 364, Basil outlined the work of the Holy Spirit. He associated the Holy Spirit with the work of *life-giving* and with the work of *perfecting.* The Spirit, the breath of God, brings things to life and brings them to completion. In Basil's theology, the life-giving role of the Spirit is evident in the sanctification of human beings, but it is also evident in the creation of the universe. Basil appealed to Psalm 33:6 to show how the Spirit is at work in creation: "By the word of the Lord the heavens were made, and all their host by the *breath* of his mouth." In both arenas, creation and sanctification, the Holy Spirit is the life-giver and the one who brings to wholeness.

Basil's great book *On the Holy Spirit* probably appeared about 375. He tells us that the occasion for writing the book was what had happened when he had made use of different versions of the trinitarian prayer of praise, the doxology:

"Lately when praying with the people, and using the full doxology to God the Father with both forms, at one time 'Glory be to the Father *with* the Son *together with* the Holy Ghost,' and at another 'Glory be to the Father *through* the Son *in* the Holy Ghost,' I was attacked by some of those present on the ground that I was introducing novel and at the same time mutually contradictory terms."[1] The attack was over Basil's use of the first form, where the Holy Spirit is glorified *with* the Father and the Son. This *with* implies equality, whereas the formula *in the Spirit* can be understood as if the Spirit is subordinate to the Father and less than fully divine. Basil tells us that because of his insistence on the legitimacy of using the preposition *with (syn)* in reference to the Spirit, he and his companions were called "innovators, revolutionizers, phrase-coiners, and every other possible name of insult."[2]

Basil vigorously defended the rightness of praying "Glory be to the Father, with *(syn)* the Son, with *(syn)* the Holy Spirit." By encouraging this form of prayer, Basil was deliberately promoting and defending the equal divinity of all three Persons of the Trinity. He had two powerful arguments in support of his position that not only the Word but also the Holy Spirit is to be glorified equally "with" the Father. The first is that, in obedience to Christ (Mt 28:19), we are baptized in the name of the Father and of the Son and of the Holy Spirit. In the baptismal faith of the Christian community the three persons are always clearly linked together. Basil concluded that to deny that the Spirit is to be glorified "with" the Father is to deny our baptism. Basil's second argument is that we are saved and deified by the Holy Spirit, and those who undermine the divinity of the Holy Spirit thereby undercut the whole theology of salvation.

In Basil's trinitarian theology, the emphasis is on the reality and significance of each Person of the Trinity. The divine union is a communion of the Persons. According to him, the "union consists in the communion *(koinōnia)* of the Godhead."[3] John Zizioulas notes that Basil's support of the word *with (syn)* in prayer, where the Father is praised "with" the Son and "with" the Spirit, causes the trinitarian relations to appear in a distinctive way: "The three persons of the Trinity appear to be equal in honour and placed one next to the other without hierarchical distinction."[4] They are understood as Persons who are "with" each other in the most profound and intimate communion. For Basil, the Holy Spirit is one who proceeds *from* the Father as principle *(arche)* and cause *(aitia),* but is also one who exists *with* the Father and the Son in radical equality and unity.[5]

Against those who would put the Spirit in a subordinate place, Basil points out that the Spirit is actually the *forerunner* to the coming of Christ and is inseparable from the works of Christ. As the forerunner the Spirit has a certain priority. In all the phases of the economy of salvation and in all the saving works of Christ the Spirit is the forerunner. Basil insists that the healings of Jesus, the exorcisms, the forgiveness of sins, our divine adoption and resurrection from the dead are all the work of the Spirit. Every phase of the divine work of our salvation is preceded by the presence and activity of the Holy Spirit.

So for Basil, when we think of the order of the Trinity from our own perspective, which is that of the economy of salvation, it is natural to begin with the Spirit, and to pass through the Son to the Father. On the other hand, if we reflect from the perspective of God's movement toward us, then we begin from the Father and think of salvation coming through the Son in the Spirit. Basil writes: "Thus the way of the knowledge of God lies from One Spirit through the One Son to the One Father, and conversely the natural Goodness and the inherent Holiness and the Royal Dignity extend from the Father through the Only-Begotten to the Spirit."[6] From one perspective we begin from the Holy Spirit and from another we begin from the Father. Basil thus anticipates the work of contemporary theologians like Jurgen Moltmann and Elizabeth Johnson, who discuss different trinitarian orders that begin with the Holy Spirit.[7] Wherever we begin, we cannot think of one Person of the Trinity acting without the others. Because of their radical communion (koinōnia) it does not matter where we begin, since we also end up with the copresence of the three Persons at once. In a letter which was formerly attributed to Basil, but which is now attributed to Gregory of Nyssa, we find the image of the chain. Drawing on the Spirit is like drawing on one end of a chain, which always brings with it the other end. In the same way, drawing on the Spirit will always draw to oneself, as well, the presence of Christ, "And since the Spirit is Christ's and of God, as Paul says, then just as one who lays hold of one end of the chain pulls the other to oneself, so one who 'draws the Spirit,' as the prophet says, draws to oneself, by means of the Spirit, both the Son and the Spirit at the same time."[8]

For Eastern theologians like Basil, as well as for those of the West, when the Trinity acts in creation it acts as one. But this does not need to rule out, as it often has in the West, a distinct and proper role of the trinitarian Persons in creation and salvation. In recent times, theologians have rightly pointed out that there is a distinctive and proper role of the Word in the Incarnation and of the Holy Spirit in our sanctification.[9] But I suggest that there is a proper role of the Holy Spirit not only in our salvation but also in the work of creation. As Rahner has said, creation and salvation are not to be understood as separate and unrelated acts of God, but as two distinct dimensions of the trinitarian God's one act of self-giving to the world.[10] If there are proper roles for the Word and the Spirit in the work of our salvation, it may well be that there are proper roles for them in the work of creation.

In the rest of this chapter I explore the distinctive role of the Holy Spirit in relation to creation through evolution, keeping in mind Basil's teaching that when one Person acts, the others act in mutual communion *(koinōnia)*. I begin from Basil's idea that the Holy Spirit is not only the Life-Giver in terms of our sanctification, but is also Life-Giver with regard to the work of creation. Then I explore this life-giving role of the Spirit, by seeing the Spirit as the power of becoming at work in evolutionary history, as the interior presence of God to all creatures, and as the ecstatic bringer of communion.

The Holy Spirit as Life-Giver

In the creed associated with the First Council of Constantinople, the words used to express the divinity of the Holy Spirit stay close to the language of the Scriptures. Following Paul (2 Cor 3:17), the Creed describes the Spirit as "Lord." Following John's Gospel (Jn 6:63), it describes the Holy Spirit as the "Life-Giver" *(Zoopoion)*.[11] The credal description of the Holy Spirit as "Life-Giver" is rich and evocative. It has obvious possibilities in the search for an understanding of the role of the Holy Spirit in relation to biological evolution.

In one of Paul's letters to the Corinthian community, we are told that "the letter kills, but the *Spirit gives life*" (2 Cor 3:6). In Romans we hear: "For the law of the *Spirit of life* in Christ Jesus has set you free from the law of sin and death" (Rom 7:2). The life-giving Spirit brings not only the new life of grace (Rom 5:5) but also the new life of bodily resurrection: "But if Christ is in you, though the body is dead because of sin, the *Spirit is life* because of righteousness. If the Spirit of him who raised Jesus from the dead dwells in you, he who raised Christ from the dead will *give life* to your mortal bodies also *through his Spirit* that dwells in you" (Rom 8:10–11). When Paul struggles to describe the resurrection from the dead he speaks of the "spirited" body, and talks of the risen Christ as the last Adam who became a "life-giving spirit" (1 Cor 15:44–45).

In John, the concept of the Spirit as "Life-Giver" appears in the discourse on the bread of life in chapter 6. Jesus' teaching on this theme creates difficulties for some of the disciples and, in this context, Jesus tells them: "It is *the spirit that gives life;* the flesh is useless. The words that I have spoken to you are spirit and life" (6:63). The contrast between spirit and flesh points back to the distinction made earlier in the Nicodemus story, between those born of the flesh and those born of the Spirit:

> Jesus answered him, "Very truly, I tell you, no one can see the kingdom of God without being born from above." Nicodemus said to him, "How can anyone be born after having grown old? Can one enter a second time into the mother's womb and be born?" Jesus answered, "Very truly, I tell you, no one can enter the kingdom of God without being born of water and Spirit. What is born of the flesh is flesh, and what is born of the Spirit is spirit. Do not be astonished that I said to you, 'You must be born from above.' The wind blows where it chooses, and you hear the sound of it,

but you do not know where it comes from or where it goes. So it is with everyone who is born of the Spirit" (Jn 3:3–8).

In the prologue to the Gospel, John has already made it clear that those who believe in the Word come among us are given power to become "children of God," children who are born not of the flesh, but "of God" (1:12–13). Here, in chapter 3 of the Gospel, the Spirit is presented to us as a mysterious life-giving mother. We are told that what is required is not a return to our human mother's womb, but a new birthing from the womb of the Holy Spirit. But this is a distinctive kind of birth, a being born into the life of the elusive and mysterious Spirit. John's Gospel makes it clear that it is those who are born "from above," of the Life-Giver, who can enter the kingdom. They are the ones who possess eternal life.

Obviously, for Paul and John, still caught up in the relatively recent experience of Jesus, the primary focus in their description of the work of the "Life-Giver" is on our salvation and *new life* in Christ. But the Bible also sees the Spirit as Life-Giver in the more fundamental sense of the giver of *biological life.* In fact the whole image of "new life" in the Spirit depends upon the biblical notion that biological life is a gift of the life-giving Spirit.

At the beginning of the first creation account in the Book of Genesis, we are told that "a wind *(ruach)* from God swept over the face of the waters" (Gn 1:2). The same Hebrew word *ruach* can mean wind, breath, or spirit. At the beginning of the creation this wind "sweeps" or "broods" over the waters of chaos. This brooding wind is the sign and the forerunner of God's creative activity, which is initiated by God's word in the next verse: "Then God said, 'Let there be light'; and there was light" (Gn 1:3). In his commentary on this passage, Basil considers the meaning of the wind that we are told "was borne" or "was brooding" over the waters:

> How then did the Spirit of God move upon the waters? The explanation that I am about to give you is not an original one, but that of a Syrian, who was as ignorant of the wisdom of this world as he was versed in the knowledge of the Truth. He said, then, that the Syriac word was more expressive, and that being more analogous to the Hebrew term, it was a nearer approach to the scriptural sense. This is the meaning of the word; by "was borne" the Syrians, he said, understand: *it cherished the nature of the waters as one sees a bird cover the eggs with her body and impart to them vital force from her own warmth.* Such is, nearly as possible, the meaning of these words—the Spirit was borne: let us understand, that is, prepared the nature of water to produce living things.[12]

Basil concludes that this is a "sufficient proof for those who ask if the Holy Spirit took an active part in the creation of the world." He has no doubt that the "wind of God" is the Holy Spirit. It is the Spirit of God who hovers over creation like a bird on her nest. He tells us that this is "the Spirit which completes the divine and blessed Trinity."[13] Contemporary biblical scholars would be more cautious about finding a developed doctrine of the Holy Spirit in this text. But Basil's image of the mother bird covering her eggs with her body and imparting life to them through her own warmth is a wonderful way of reading Genesis 1:2. It gives vivid and rich insight into the Christian idea of the Spirit of God as Life-Giver. The Spirit broods over the waters to enable them to bring forth living creatures.[14]

In the Bible, the Breath of God is the principle of life for all living things. All things survive because God gives them the divine *ruach.* God formed the first human from the dust of the ground and breathed into this earthling's nostrils "the breath of life" (Gn 2:7). It is this breath of God that kept mortals alive for their allotted span (Gn 6:3). God threatened that the flood will "destroy from under heaven all flesh in which is the breath of life" (Gn 6:17). Those that were to be saved went into the ark with Noah "two of all flesh in which there is the breath of life" (Gn 7:15). In the Book of Job we find Job crying out: "The Spirit of God has made me, and the breath of the Almighty gives me life" (Jb 33:4). And Job declares of all living things: "If he should take back his spirit to himself, and gather to himself his breath, all flesh would perish together, and all mortals return to dust" (Jb 34:14–15; cf. Eccl 12:7). In the great scene in Ezekiel, the valley of dry bones can only be brought to life by the breath from God. The prophet is instructed: "Prophesy to the breath, prophesy, mortal and say to the breath: Thus says the Lord God: Come from the four winds, O breath, and breathe on these slain that they live" (Ez 37:9).

In Judith we find the prayer: "Let all creatures serve you, because you spoke, and they were made. You sent forth your spirit and it formed them" (Jdt 16:14). The cosmic role of the divine Spirit appears in several places in the Wisdom of Solomon: "Because the spirit of the Lord has filled the world, and that which holds all things together knows what is said" (Wis 1:7); "For your immortal spirit is in all things" (Wis 12:1). In the Psalms, the word of God and the breath of God are linked together as creative forces: "By the word of the Lord the heavens were made, and all their host by the breath of his mouth" (Ps 33:6). In Psalm 104, the great song of creation, we find the Psalmist singing of God's creatures:

These all look to you
to give them their food in due season;
when you give it to them, they gather it up;
when you open your hand, they are filled with good things.
When you hide your face, they are dismayed;
when you take away their breath, they die
and return to the dust.
When you send forth your spirit,
they are created;
and you renew the face of the ground (Ps 104:27–30).

In the biblical tradition, the breath of God is what keeps creatures alive. It is the sending forth of God's breath that creates and renews all things that exist on the face of the Earth. Creation and renewal of creation are the works of the life-giving Spirit. This general biblical concept of the Spirit as the Life-Giver provides an initial response to the question about the relation of the Holy Spirit to evolution. But this initial concept needs further specification if we are to conclude that there is a distinctive role of the Holy Spirit in biological evolution. Is the Spirit the Life-Giver in a distinctive way in relation to the other trinitarian persons? In the next sections of this chapter, I attempt to specify what is distinctive to the Spirit as the Bringer of Life.

The Life-Giving Spirit as the Power of Becoming in Evolutionary History

Christian theology has always understood that all creaturely existence is contingent upon God's continuing creation. Things exist only because God, absolute being, conserves them in their being and in their action. All creatures owe their existence at every moment to the ongoing creative activity of God. What is new in our time is the need to understand this ongoing creative activity of God in relationship to the theory of evolution.

Karl Rahner has pointed out that in evolution there are certain points where we have the appearance of what is substantially "new." The emergence of life is an example of one such an event, and another is the emergence of self-conscious human creatures. Rahner believes that such evolutionary events spring from inner-worldly causes, and that it is the work of science to explain these causes. He rejects the notion of "occasionalism," the idea that God, at certain points, intervenes as one cause amongst others to bring about a new direction.

Nevertheless, the advent of what is radically new in evolution needs accounting for, not only at the level of science, but at the deeper level of God's action in creation. How are we to understand God's ongoing creative role in the evolution of life? Rahner suggests the notion of "active self-transcendence."[15] By this he means that God is interiorly present to evolving creatures, not simply enabling them to *exist* in a static way, but enabling them to *transcend* what they already are. God enables them not only to be, but also to become something more than they are. The power of self-transcendence comes from *within* the creature, but it is a power that finally comes not from the creature, but from the ongoing creative activity of God. God upholds and empowers the process of evolution from within, as the power enabling creation itself to bring about something new. This means that when something new emerges in evolution, at one level it will be the effect of finite causes, such as genetic mutation and natural selection. But at another level, evolutionary change is the effect of God's creative activity, working through the power of self-transcendence from within the creatures. God, then, does not "intervene" as one cause among others but is always present as dynamic absolute Being, which enables creatures not only to exist but also to transcend themselves and to become what is new.

Rahner has discussed this idea particularly in his evolutionary Christology.[16] He sees human beings as the self-transcendence of matter into self-consciousness before God. He sees Jesus as the one in whom the self-transcendence of the universe toward God reaches its final and irrevocable stage. He is both the self-transcendence of the universe to God and God's absolute self-communication to creation. I find Rahner's thought rich and stimulating, and believe it can be developed by adding the idea that *the process of self-transcendence can be seen as the work of the Holy Spirit,* in and through whom the triune God is immanent in all things. Basil, echoing the Scriptures, describes the Spirit as the Life-Giver and the one who brings to wholeness. In an evolutionary framework, I would suggest that it is the life-giving and completing Spirit who is the power that enables creatures to transcend themselves. It is the Life-Giver who enables the movement of the unfolding of the early universe from the Big Bang, the beginning of nuclear processes in stars, the formation of our planetary system, the emergence of life on Earth, and the evolution of self-conscious human beings. It is this same Spirit who empowers the life and ministry of Jesus of Nazareth within our evolutionary and cultural history as the radically Spirit-filled human being.

The Spirit is not a power that can be discovered among the forces of the universe. The laws and forces of nature have their own integrity. The action of the Life-Giver is at another level. Walter Kasper has pointed out that, at this level, it is the Holy Spirit who is ultimately the source of all novelty in creation:

But the Spirit is also the source of movement and life in the created world. Whenever something new arises, whenever life is awakened and reality reaches ecstatically beyond itself, in all seeking and striving, in every ferment and birth, and even more in the beauty of creation, something of the being and activity of God's Spirit is manifested.[17]

The Spirit of God is the Life-Giver, the power of becoming, who enables the unfolding of the universe and the evolution of life on Earth. Yves Congar reflects on the Spirit secretly guiding God's work in the world with the aid of words from the medieval Persian mystic Rumi (d. 1273):

> Know that it is waves of Love that make the wheel of the heavens turn.
> Without Love, the world would not be animated.
> How can an inorganic thing be transformed into a plant?
> How can vegetable things sacrifice themselves so as to be endowed with spirit?
> How could that spirit sacrifice itself for that Breath, an expiration of which made Mary pregnant?…
> Every atom is seized by that Perfection and hastens towards it.…
> That haste says implicitly: "Glory be to God."[18]

As Congar notes, it was only a generation later that the European poet Dante would end his *Paradiso* with the words:

> Here my strength was not enough for the sublime vision,
> but already, like a wheel moving steadily round,
> my desire and my will were directed by
> The Love that moves the Sun and the other stars.[19]

The Holy Spirit is the life-giving "Love that moves the Sun and other stars." It is the Spirit who is at work in the evolution of life on Earth over the last three and a half billion years. It is this same Spirit which empowers the incarnation and animates Jesus of Nazareth in his life, death, and resurrection. Looking back on the whole sweep of evolutionary emergence we can say with Rumi: "Every atom is seized by that Perfection and hastens towards it."

The Life-Giving Spirit as Interior Presence

In attempting to articulate the role of the Holy Spirit in the evolution of life, I have suggested that the Spirit is to be understood as the Life-Giver who empowers the becoming of creation. A further dimension and specification of the Spirit's role has to do with the immanence and interiority of the Spirit to all creatures.

At the heart of Christian faith is the conviction that the God who radically transcends creation is also intimately present to every creature. Augustine speaks of the divine presence as *interior intimo meo*—as closer to me than I am to myself. God is present to human creatures in an interpersonal way through the gift of grace. But this same God is present interiorly to every creature by the relationship of ongoing creation.

Traditionally, theology has used the language of divine "omnipresence" and of divine "immensity" to describe God's presence to all of creation. In terms of our contemporary understanding of our universe, this traditional teaching would mean that God is present to every particle of every one of the more than a hundred billion galaxies that make up our known universe. God is interiorly and intimately present in all that God creates.

Since the time of Gregory the Great, God's presence to creatures has been distinguished into three different modes:

(1) God is present through essence *(per essentiam)* insofar as God continually creates things by giving them their being; (2) God is present through power *(per potentiam)* in that God empowers creatures to act; (3) God is present as all embracing knowledge *(per praesentiam)* in that God sees the being and activity of creatures.[20] But, of course, these are different ways of reflecting about the one simple presence of the triune God to each and every creature.

In the Bible, this interior divine presence is related to the life-giving Spirit. This theme is expressed with great religious feeling in Psalm 139:

> Where can I go from your spirit?
> Or where can I flee from your presence?
> If I ascend to heaven you are there;
> if I make my bed in Sheol you are there.
> If I take the wings of the morning
> and settle at the farthest limits of the sea,
> even there your hand shall lead me,
> and your right hand shall hold me fast.
> If I say, "Surely darkness shall cover me,
> and the light around me become night,"
> even the darkness is not dark to you;
> the night is bright as the day,
> for darkness is as light to you. (Ps 139:7–12)

I have already drawn attention to the texts in the Wisdom of Solomon where we are told that "the spirit of the Lord has filled the world" and that "the one who holds all things together hears every sound" (Wis 1:7). Then, later in the same book, we read:

> Because the whole world before you is like a speck that tips the scales,
> and like a drop of morning dew that falls on the ground.

But you are merciful to all, for you can do all things,
and you overlook peoples' sins, so that they may repent.
For *you love all things that exist*,
and detest none of the things that you have made,
for you would not have made anything if you had hated it.
How would anything have endured if you had not willed it?
Or how would anything not called forth from you have
been preserved?
You spare all things, for they are yours, O Lord, *you who love
    the living.*
For *your immortal spirit is in all things.* (Wis 11:22–12:1)

The God who "loves the living" dwells in all creatures
through the Spirit. The Creator Spirit is present in every
flower, bird, and human being, in every quasar and in every
atomic particle, closer to them than they are to themselves,
enabling them to be and to become. As Jurgen Moltmann has
said: "The operations of God's life-giving and life-affirming
Spirit are universal and can be recognized in everything
which ministers to life and resists its destruction."[21]

Elizabeth Johnson has shown how the destructive
exploitation of the Earth and the marginalization of women
are both intrinsically related to "forgetting the Creator
Spirit who pervades the world in the dance of life."[22] She
points toward an alternative healing vision in which dam-
aging dualisms are transcended. It is by remembering the
interiority and presence of the Spirit to all things that we
can find freedom from dualism categories, and find life in
the vision of the Creator Spirit enfolding a reconciled community of women and men, and a healed community of life
on Earth. Johnson sees the Spirit as "life that gives life":

She is radiant life energy that like wind, fire, and water
awakens and enlivens all things. Each of these symbols has
a numinous quality that evokes better than abstract words

the presence of the Creator Spirit in the world, moving over the void, breathing into the chaos, pouring out, informing, quickening, warming, setting free, blessing, dancing in mutual immanence with the world.[23]

It is the Creator Spirit who is the divine presence deep down in all things. It is this intimate presence that is not only the source of all life, but the power that enables creatures to transcend themselves in evolutionary change.

The Life-Giving Spirit as Ecstatic Communion

I have been suggesting that the Holy Spirit is the Life-Giver, the dynamism of self-transcendence within creation, more interior to things than they are to themselves. Now I suggest a further depth to this description of the Spirit at work in ongoing creation. The Spirit is the life-giving, immanent dynamism of evolutionary process, precisely because the Spirit is the *ecstatic one*, who in the divine choice to create goes beyond the divine communion to what is not divine, and brings what is not divine into relation with the divine Persons. The Spirit as the excess, the ecstasy, of divine love, brings creation into relationship with the divine life. It is this ongoing relationship that enables creatures to exist and to become. The Spirit, present to every creature, brings every part of our universe into a creaturely communion with God. The Spirit is the ecstatic gift of divine communion with creatures, whereby each creature exists, and whereby each creature is caught up with the dynamism of the trinitarian *perichōrēsis*.

The Spirit is the ecstatic gift of communion only in profound unity with the other divine Persons. But, nevertheless, this work of communion-making between creatures and the trinitarian God can be understood as a *proper* role of the Holy Spirit. It is not simply that this work is appropriated to the Holy Spirit. It can be thought of as proper, because it is an overflow into creation of what distinguishes the Holy Spirit within the trinitarian dynamic. Within the trinitarian relations, the Person of the Holy Spirit represents the ecstasy and the excess of divine love. Because of the Spirit, the divine life of love cannot be thought of as a self-sufficient love between two Persons. In the Trinity love breaks beyond itself to involve the one whom Richard of St. Victor called the *condilectus,* the one who shares in love for the beloved and is loved with the beloved. The Holy Spirit makes it impossible for the love of the Trinity to be thought of as simply a face-to-face love of two Persons. The Spirit expresses the dynamism and abundance of the divine communion. In the free divine choice to create a universe of creatures, it is the Spirit's role to be the dynamic and free overflow of divine communion that embraces the creatures. As Christian Duquoc has said, the Holy Spirit makes the divine communion open to what is not divine. The Spirit is the indwelling of God where God is, is in one sense, *outside* God's self.[24] The Spirit is God's *ecstasy* directed toward what is God's *other*, the creature.

Yves Congar, in his three-volume work on the Holy Spirit, sees the Holy Spirit as *absolute Gift.*[25] The Spirit is the Gift of love and of divine communion *(koinōnia)* directed toward creation. Congar points out that the Holy Spirit is always understood as a "going out," an "impulse," an "ecstasy." Following Duquoc, he sees the Spirit as God *outside* God's self, God in creatures, God in us. Congar sums this up with the idea that God is Love and Grace, and says that "Love and Grace are hypostatized in the Spirit."[26] This means, he writes, that the "Holy Spirit, who is the term of

96

the communication of the divine life *intra deum,* is the principle of this communication of God outside himself and beyond himself."[27] The logic of this for me is the conclusion, which Congar does not draw, that to be the ecstatic divine presence in creation, bringing all creatures into communion with the trinitarian communion, is *distinctively* and *properly* the role of the Holy Spirit.

Paul tells us that "God's love has been poured into our hearts through the Holy Spirit that has been given to us" (Rom 5:5). This ecstatic Gift dwelling in us takes us into the divine *koinōnia:* "When we cry, 'Abba! Father!' it is that very Spirit bearing witness with our spirit that we are children of God" (Rom 8:15–16). At the end of 2 Corinthians, Paul prays for the community: "The grace of the Lord Jesus Christ, the love of God, and the communion (*koinōnia*) of the Holy Spirit be with you all" (2 Cor 13:13). For Paul, this communion of the Holy Spirit is the life that the Christian community shares, as a reflection and participation of the divine life through the gift of the indwelling Spirit. This redemptive and liberating *koinōnia* is a central dimension of Christian life. It also is a pledge and foretaste of the reconciliation and communion of all things in Christ (Rom 8:18–23).

But what of nonhuman creatures? Is the communion of the Holy Spirit something that other creatures participate in only through human beings? I have been arguing that this communion is something that all creatures already share by virtue of being God's creatures, through the ongoing action of the Spirit in the relation of continual creation. Jurgen Moltmann rightly insists that the redeeming Spirit of Christ and the creative life-giving Spirit of God are one and the same. The *koinōnia* of the Holy Spirit embraces not just human beings, but all of God's creatures, creation in all its complexity.

For Moltmann, then, the experience of the Holy Spirit in the community of the church "leads of itself beyond the limits of the church to the rediscovery of the same Spirit in nature, in plants, in animals, and in the ecosystems of the earth."[28] The experience of the Spirit in the church carries Christianity beyond itself to the greater community of all God's creatures. Moltmann can say, then, that "the community of creation, in which all created things exist with one another, for one another and in one another, is also the fellowship of the Holy Spirit."[29] Moltmann sees creation as "aligned towards community" and as "created in the form of communities." He sees it as appropriate to talk about a "community of creation" and to recognize the operation of the life-giving Spirit of God in the trend toward relationship in created things.[30] He suggests that this community of creation, which is inspired by the Holy Spirit, is meant to lead through evolutionary history, neither to simple diversity nor to simple unity, but to "differentiated community that liberates the individual members belonging to it."[31] This suggests that Christians, who believe that they are caught up in the personal and ecclesial *koinonia* of the Holy Spirit, will see themselves linked in relationships of kinship and community with all other creatures in a global *koinonia* of the Holy Spirit.

I have been suggesting that the Holy Spirit has a particular role in creation, and, more specifically, in the history of biological evolution: the Spirit is the *Life-Giver*, the *Power of Becoming*, the *Interior Presence of God*, the ecstatic *Communion-Bringer*. As I insisted previously, where the Spirit is, there also are the other Persons in the divine Communion that is the being of God. The Spirit always unites creatures in Christ, in communion with the one who is the Fountain Fullness from which all things come.

Congar has said that "the Spirit is without a face and almost without a name."[32] Many theologians point to the shadowy nature of our understanding of the Holy Spirit. The Spirit is described as the "anonymous" or the "unknown" Person of the Trinity. This is often interpreted positively as related to the transparency of the Spirit in leading us to the other Persons of the Trinity. But I believe that this line of thought can be taken too far, and can lead to a diminished notion of the Person of the Holy Spirit.

In the economy, we experience Jesus as the "human face" of God and, in so doing, our experience of divine revelation in Jesus Christ points to something of the nature of the eternal Word and Wisdom of God. We do *not* experience the Spirit as "human face" of God. But we *do* experience the Spirit as the "inexpressible closeness" of God.[33] And what must be said is that this closeness is not *less* than personal, and certainly not *less* than human, but is a personal presence that *abundantly transcends* the human. If Jesus is the face of God in our midst, God in human form, the Spirit is God present in a thousand ways in and beyond the limits of the human. In Jesus, God is revealed in specific human historical shape. In the Spirit, God is given to us in a personal presence which transcends human limits.

We can become aware of the Holy Spirit, as the unspeakable closeness of God, in silence before the mystery of the universe that opens up before us with the aid of the Hubble telescope, in delight in the flashing colors of a parrot on the wing, in the exuberant experience of sunshine on a day in spring, in the experience of mutual friendship, in finding that there is a holy presence with us in times of suffering and grief, and even in what seems at first like nothing but absence and abandonment. It is the Spirit who stirs within us in the experience of faith in the Gospel, in our participation in the eucharistic communion of the church, in the sense of global solidarity with all human beings and with all God's creatures, and in our union with Jesus before the One he called *Abba* and who can also be called our beloved Mother. The Holy Spirit is inexpressible personal closeness in all these ways and in many others.

I believe that it can be said that these experiences of the Holy Spirit in the economy of salvation point to the sheer abundance, to the ecstatic character of the Person of the Holy Spirit in the trinitarian relations. The Holy Spirit is not less than humanly personal, but inexpressibly and abundantly more. This same Spirit is the Life-Giver, the Interior Presence of the Divine, the Power of Self-Transcendence, the Ecstatic Gift of Communion, who enables creatures to exist and enables evolutionary emergence to occur.

6 *Evolution and Jesus, the Wisdom of God*

THE EVOLUTIONARY WORLDVIEW IS AN OVERARCHING and total one. For those who have allowed it to shape their consciousness, it becomes a radically new frame of reference, a way of thinking about the unfolding of the universe and the emergence of life on Earth which is quite different from all pre-evolutionary views.

Most Christians see Jesus of Nazareth as central to their worldview. They believe that Jesus has meaning not just for human existence in the world, but in some way for the whole of reality. For those, like myself, who hold this view and also accept an evolutionary worldview, a key question for contemporary theology becomes: How can we think of the meaning of Jesus Christ within an evolutionary framework?

In this chapter I respond to this question with a Wisdom Christology. As a first step, I look briefly at the evolutionary Christologies developed by Teilhard de Chardin, Karl Rahner, and Jurgen Moltmann. Then I attempt to integrate elements of these views within an evolutionary Wisdom Christology.

Teilhard de Chardin (1881–1955)

In *The Phenomenon of Man,* Teilhard de Chardin's thought moves in a great drama of evolution from matter to life, from life to self-conscious thinking creatures, and from self-conscious thinking creatures to the convergence of consciousness in what he calls the "Omega Point." His most fundamental affirmation is that, just as the universe is engaged in a process of cosmic expansion, so it is also

101

engaged in a movement of increasing complexity. This complexity is bound up with an increase in interiorization, an increase of consciousness. Teilhard sees this trend toward increasing complexity and consciousness as a universal law, a law that he finds empirically evident from his study of evolutionary history.[1]

He sees human beings as prime participants in this evolutionary movement, because, at this current stage of evolutionary history, the most important increase in complexity occurs in human thought and culture. Teilhard calls this dimension of our evolutionary history the "noosphere." The living world of plants and animals that inhabit the Earth has long been thought of as a "biosphere," a layer of life around the global "geosphere." With the emergence of human consciousness we have the emergence of a new layer, a "thinking layer." Teilhard tells us, that with the noosphere, the Earth "gets a new skin" and "finds its soul."[2]

Christopher Mooney points out that Teilhard connects evolution and Christ as the Omega Point by means of three distinct but related levels of argument.[3] First there is a *scientific* argument, built on observation of the pattern of evolution. In the history of evolution, Teilhard finds the law of complexity-consciousness at work. It is this that gives rise to the true becoming of the universe, which he calls "cosmogenesis." A study of this process leads Teilhard to project forward into its future. He suggests that, after perhaps millions of years, humankind will be able to cross a new threshold of reflection and enter into a single collectivity of consciousness, the Omega Point.

At a second level, Teilhard moves to a more *philosophical* argument. He begins from his conviction that evolutionary progress now takes the shape of higher forms of interpersonal communion. This leads Teilhard to argue for the need for a divine Center, an Omega who is a personal source and object of love, capable of motivating the human community to develop a capacity for a love that will come to embrace the whole world. This Center, he argues, would have to be a personal reality already at work in the world, radiating and activating the love energy of the universe.[4]

The third argument is a *theological* one. At this level of his discussion, Teilhard draws directly on Christian revelation, and sees the Jesus Christ of revelation as the true Omega of evolution. The goal and the convergence of the process of evolution are found in the Christ of the resurrection, the Christ who will come again in the parousia.[5] For Teilhard, the phenomenological and philosophical levels of analysis are brought into a unity with the data of revelation to form his Christology, in which the risen Christ is the Prime Mover of evolution, the one who actuates the energies of the universe. Cosmogenesis now takes on the shape of the Word incarnate. This leads Teilhard to speak of a genesis which is truly *Christic*, which he calls a "Christogenesis."

At the heart of Teilhard's concept of Christogenesis is the idea that the Body of Christ forms the personal center for humankind and for the whole of physical reality. He sees this as the same bodily being, Jesus of Nazareth, who lived and died at a particular time in history. It is this same Christ who has now become the universal Christ, the one center of the one supernaturally graced universe. Teilhard insists that Christ is the physical center. In his *Le Milieu divin,* it is clear that it is Christ who is the omnipresent "milieu" and "center," radiating the energy that leads the universe to its culmination in God. Teilhard takes the traditional teaching about God's interior presence to all things (divine "immensity") and applies it to the risen Christ. Through the incarnation, he tells us "the divine immensity has transformed itself for us into the omnipresence of Christification."[6]

Teilhard sees this omnipresence of Christ as a prolongation of the eucharistic presence of Christ. For him, the eucharist is the expression of the divine energy applying itself little by little to every atom of the universe. The eucharistic transformation goes beyond and completes the transubstantiation of bread and wine. In a secondary but true sense, the earthly elements consecrated are not simply the bread and wine but "are formed by the totality of the world and the duration of creation is needed for its consecration."[7]

In his thought on the redemption, Teilhard's emphasis is very much on developing a positive view of the Redeemer in terms of evolutionary history. He has little to say about the atonement and forgiveness of sin. He suggests that Christ the *Redeemer* will "ultimately be seen in the fullness of his power as Christ the *Evolver*."[8] His focus is not so much on Christ bearing the sins of a guilty world as on Christ "bearing the weight of a world in the course of evolution."[9]

The role of the church is crucial. It is called to be a "phylum of love" within the noosphere. The church has the fundamental task of giving expression to the Christic energy of charity for the world. The parousia can take place only at the point of "planetary maturation." This will be an event that is not within our history but at its end. This maturation can occur through the progress of human evolution, on the one hand, and by the inner transformation of the process by divine love, on the other. In Teilhard's view, this cannot be completed without the animating action of the church, the phylum of love within the community of creation.

Karl Rahner (1904–1984)

At the beginning of his "Christology Within an Evolutionary View of the World," Karl Rahner notes that his intention is to avoid Teilhard's theories and to work only with the theology that any theologian might use. Rahner presupposes an evolutionary view of the world and asks whether Christology is compatible with it. He makes it clear that he does not want to try to deduce the Christian doctrine of the incarnation from an evolutionary view. What he wants to do is to show whether there is any "intrinsic affinity" and any possibility of "reciprocal correlation" between an evolutionary view of the world and Christology.[10]

Rahner begins his reflections from the fundamental unity he finds in all created things. All of creation is united in its one *origin* from God, in its one *self-realization* through ongoing creation and in its one *future* in God. As for human beings, Rahner argues that we form a unity, which is prior to the differentiation in ourselves between the elements of matter and spirit. He sees us as experiencing both ourselves and the world around us as *matter,* insofar as we encounter other individual and distinct beings in our world. We experience ourselves as *spirit,* insofar as in these encounters we become conscious of ourselves in self-presence, and this occurs by reason of our openness to infinite mystery.

Like Teilhard de Chardin, Rahner considers the transitions whereby matter becomes life and life becomes self-conscious spirit. He suggests that it is the intrinsic nature of matter to develop toward spirit. He sees the human being as the self-transcendence of matter. In the evolutionary developments that take place from matter to life, and from life to self-consciousness, creatures achieve something new, something that did not exist before. Rahner sees this as implying

105

a power of self-transcendence that is truly intrinsic to the creature, but which occurs through the creative power of the absolute being of God. According to Rahner, matter comes to consciousness in human beings. Nature finds itself in the human person and in the human community. Rahner writes: "The one material cosmos is the single body as it were of a multiple self-presence of this very cosmos and its orientation towards its absolute and infinite ground."[11] The human being, then, can be understood as the universe come to self-awareness in a particular time and place.

Rahner sees the universe as borne from its very beginning by a thrust toward an ever closer and more conscious relationship to its Creator. The goal of this whole movement is immediacy between God and the universe, communion between God and conscious creatures, and, through them, with the whole universe. The goal of the world is God's self-communication with it. This is what we human beings call our final salvation. But, Rahner insists, final salvation is also the final and definitive state of fulfillment of the whole cosmos. We experience only the very beginning of the movement toward this goal. But amidst all the ambiguity of our finitude and sin we already experience God's self-communication in grace. This experience of grace occurs in moments when we encounter transcendence and mystery at the heart of life. We can freely say "Yes" to the mysterious presence and self-communication of God. In this event of grace, we can find the foretaste and promise of our union with God in glory, the union that will involve the transformation of the whole of reality in God.

Jesus Christ is the absolute guarantee that the ultimate self-transcendence of creation into God will succeed. It has already begun with him. In Jesus we find the "initial beginning and definitive triumph of the movement of the world's self-transcendence into absolute closeness to the mystery of God."[12] Jesus *is* the self-transcendence of the universe into God. But God's self-communication is addressed to human beings in their common history. As historical human beings, we look for an unambiguous historical self-communication from God. This is what we actually find in the history of Jesus of Nazareth. Jesus is not only the self-transcendence of the universe to God; he is at the same time God's historical self-communication to us. Because he is both, Rahner sees Jesus Christ as the "absolute savior." This does not mean that salvation begins with him in a temporal sense. Rather, Rahner sees salvation and grace as coextensive with world history. But God's universal saving love finds explicit and irreversible expression in Jesus Christ. This savior is the one in whom God's self-communication exists irrevocably, can be recognized unambiguously as irrevocable, and reaches its climax within human history. This point is not the conclusion of God's self-communication—this will come only in God's final eschatological action. But Jesus is the unambiguous and irreversible beginning of God's final salvation.

In this savior, there is on the one hand the irreversible self-communication of God to creatures. And on the other hand there is the definitive human acceptance of this communication. When both of these occur in Jesus of Nazareth, there is present in human history an absolute self-communication on both sides. In Jesus, God gives God's self to the evolving world in love definitely and irrevocably; and in Jesus, the evolving creation accepts God definitively and irrevocably.

Rahner sees creation and incarnation as united in one great act of divine self-communication. Creation can be seen as a "partial moment in the process in which God becomes world." God always intended to give God's self to us in the very process of the historical self-transcendence of the universe into God. We can understand creation and incarnation "as two moments and two phases of the *one* process of God's self-giving and self-expression, although it is an intrinsically differentiated process."[13]

Jurgen Moltmann (1926–)

Jurgen Moltmann, in *The Way of Jesus Christ* (1990), sets out to construct a postmodern, ecological Christology. In this book, Moltmann enters into dialogue with the messianic perspective of Jewish thinkers, and builds on his own earlier work on the cross and the eschatological resurrection of Christ.[14] In the last part of this new book he focuses his attention on the "Cosmic Christ."[15]

Moltmann points out that we need to go beyond modern Christologies, which focus on human beings, to a postmodern Christology in the framework of nature. He draws attention to the cosmic Christology of Colossians and Ephesians. In them Christ is presented as redeemer with regard to the cosmos as it was understood in the first century, a world populated by angelic and demonic powers. In our own time, Moltmann tells us, theology must again confront Christ the redeemer with the natural world, but this time it is a world that humans have poisoned and condemned to death. The original biblical Christology presents us with the means to do this with its vision of the "always greater" Christ, the Christ of nature and of the universe. Moltmann shows that this original biblical cosmic theology of Christ is achieved by means of a wisdom Christology, building on texts such as chapter 8 of Proverbs. He argues that in the early Christian understanding, the redeeming death of Christ had a *cosmic* function. Jesus died for the reconciliation of the cosmos (2 Cor 5:19). The world is understood to be in need of redemption. Moltmann points out that while Paul understands Christ's redemption of creation as "not yet," in Colossians and Ephesians it tends to be seen as something that is "already" at work.

What is needed today, Moltmann argues, is a *differentiated* cosmic Christology. Christ's role with regard to creation needs to be understood in three distinct but interrelated strands: (1) Christ as the *ground* of the creation of all things *(creatio originalis);* (2) Christ as the *moving power* in the evolution of creation *(creatio continua);* (3) Christ as the *redeemer* of the whole creation process *(creatio nova)*. It is the third of these that Moltmann believes has been most neglected. It is here that he places his own emphasis.

Moltmann considers the contributions of Teilhard de Chardin and Karl Rahner, to show how the elements of truth he finds in them can be absorbed into a differentiated Christology. He criticizes Teilhard for, among other things, overlooking the problem of evil, particularly the ambiguity and cruelty of evolution itself. He sees Teilhard's "Christ the Evolver" as a story of winners. Above all, he finds in Teilhard no theology of the redemption of evolution and its victims: "If Christ is to be thought of in conjunction with evolution, then he must become evolution's redeemer."[16] The criticisms Moltmann makes of Rahner are similar. He finds that Rahner fails to draw attention to evolution's victims. He suggests that Rahner's anthropocentrism fails to incorporate the cosmos and a real respect for nature. Rahner presupposes an evolutionary view, without adopting it in a critical way. He fails to uncover its tragic side. Christ is seen as the summit of evolutionary development, but not as the redeemer of the development from its ambiguities. Nevertheless, Moltmann clearly accepts Rahner's concept of evolutionary self-transcendence when it is joined with the theology of Christ as the redeemer of evolution.[17]

Moltmann's own emphasis, then, is on Christ as the redeemer of evolution. Is it conceivable, he asks, that God's future for creation, God's final salvation, will be achieved by way of evolution or self-transcendence? Moltmann's answer is "No," because, he says, evolution takes place in time and does not lead to the immortality of individual creatures. Their salvation is conceivable only as an eschatological event. He sees the eschatological movement of redemption as running *counter* to evolution. The raising of the dead, the gathering of the victims, and the seeking of the lost bring a redemption of the world that no evolution can ever achieve. God's salvation can come only eschatologically as a "new creation," the "bringing back of all things out of their past, and the gathering of them into the kingdom of glory," the "raising of the dead and the whole of nature."[18]

God's eschatological future, Moltmann insists, must be understood *diachronically:* simultaneous to all things, and representing eternity to all things. It is a waking and a gathering of every creature of every time. The kingdom of God is not the goal *(telos)* of the historical process, but the *end.* As the end of time "the parousia comes to all times simultaneously in a single instant."[19] The evolutionary series is the outcome of God's *continuous creation.* Redemption, God's *new creation,* can come only from the coming of Christ in glory. Our experience of evolutionary self-transcendence can be understood only as parables, hints, anticipations and preparations, and heralds of this new creation.

Moltmann's cosmic Christology leads to ethical conclusions. Reconciliation in Christ must lead to reconciliation with all God's creatures. Our relationship with other creatures needs to be based on a recognition of their dignity before God, on God's love directed toward them, on Christ's giving of himself for them, and on the indwelling of the Holy Spirit in them. Such an approach leads to the perception of the rights of individual creatures within the community of creation. Moltmann argues for a community of human beings, plants, and animals *based upon law.* All animal and plant species have their own rights, and these must be observed. This idea of the community of creation based on law has its roots in the Sabbath and the Sabbath year. Human beings do not "own" other creatures. They have only a limited right to use them within the framework of God's peace. In this framework, the extermination of whole species of plant and animal life must be viewed as a "sacrilege."[20] Human beings are obliged to protect other species. They have responsibility toward other human beings, including those who are still to come, and they have a responsibility to other creatures that share the Earth with them.

Reflections

I find Teilhard's vision a magnificent one. At the heart of the vision is the idea of Christ the Omega, who is not simply identified with biological evolution (as Moltmann seems to suggest), but who is the transcendent source and goal of evolutionary movement. I value the way Teilhard makes a theological link between the risen Christ and matter, through the union between Jesus Christ beyond death and the divine presence to all things. But, in the light of the atrocities of the twentieth century, I am not able to be as optimistic about evolutionary unfolding as Teilhard was. This reservation applies above all to the unfolding of cultural evolution, the noosphere. Teilhard's theology is clearly in need of development at certain points—above all, his view of sin and redemption from sin.

Although Karl Rahner has often written on eschatology, his focus in his evolutionary Christology is not on the Omega Point of Teilhard de Chardin. Rather, Rahner looks back on the whole sweep of evolutionary history, from matter to life to self-consciousness, to the historical event of Jesus of Nazareth two thousand years ago and our ongoing story today. His contribution is to see Jesus Christ as both the self-transcendence of the evolutionary universe to God and as God's self-communication to the universe. Moltmann finds Rahner's theology too anthropocentric. I would respond that Rahner's theology is far more concerned with the physical universe than Moltmann allows, but in the light of the ecological crisis we face, needs further development to bring out its ecological consequences and to escape the charge of anthropocentrism. It is clear that in his original work on evolutionary Christology, Rahner does not come to terms with the elements of unpredictability and chance that are taken for granted in contemporary theories of evolution. In his later work, however, he acknowledges these issues more clearly.[21]

Moltmann argues that both Teilhard and Rahner ignore the "victims" of evolution. I wonder if it is helpful to think of creatures that have died as food for others, of creatures that belong to now extinct species, as "victims." Do we need to think of bacteria that lived two billion years ago as victims in need of individual redemption? Does each dinosaur need redemption, or did they each find dinosaur fulfillment in their life span? I do not think the answers to these questions are obvious. All living creatures die. Does this make them victims? As I have said earlier in this work,

I do not think it is helpful theology to make such a contrast between God's work in creation through evolutionary process, which involves natural selection, and God's work in redemption, which according to Moltmann, runs counter to natural selection.

Moltmann's insistence on the need for redemption from the ambiguities of evolutionary history and his emphasis on the ecological consequences of a cosmic Christology are his central contributions to an evolutionary Christology. I agree with his insistence on the divine redemptive act. But must this be thought of as a divine eschatological act occurring only at the end of time (Moltmann's view), or can we think of God's saving action occurring in and through the process of self-transcendence of the universe (Rahner's view)? My own tendency in the Wisdom Christology that follows is to hold together creation and salvation in the way that Rahner suggests.

Jesus as the Wisdom of God

In this final section, I attempt to build on the insights of Teilhard, Rahner, and Moltmann, by way of a return to a biblical Wisdom Christology.[22] For the sake of clarity and brevity, I proceed schematically by making a series of six statements and commenting on them.

1. *According to the Jewish Wisdom Literature, Sophia, the Wisdom of God, who makes her home among us, is God's companion in creating all things.*

In the biblical Wisdom books, Sophia, the personification of Wisdom, is consistently associated with God's work of creation. In Job, we hear that only God knows the way to

Wisdom. We are told that when God established the weight of the wind, the measure of the waters, and made a decree for the rain and the thunderbolt, God saw, declared and established, and searched out Wisdom (Jb 28:20–28). In Proverbs, Sophia speaks in her own voice of her role in creation. She tells us that she was brought forth at the beginning, as the first of God's acts of long ago, before the depths, the springs, the mountains, and before the earth and all its fields. She was there when God established the heavens and set boundaries for the sea. When God marked out the foundations of the earth, she was beside God "like a master worker." She was daily God's "delight," rejoicing before God and always, "rejoicing in the inhabited world and delighting in the human race" (8:22–31). In Sirach, Sophia says of herself: "I came forth from the mouth of the most high and covered the earth like a mist. I dwelt in the highest heaven, and my throne was a pillar of cloud. Alone I compassed the vault of heaven and traversed the depths of the abyss. Over waves of the sea, over all the earth, and over every people and nation I have held sway" (24:3–6). In the Wisdom of Solomon, Sophia is described as the "mother" of all good things (7:12) and as the "fashioner of all things" (7:22). She is called a "reflection of eternal light, a spotless mirror of the working of God, and an image of the divine goodness" (7:26). We are told that Sophia "can do all things" and that she "renews all things" (7:27). She "reaches mightily from one end of the earth to the other and she orders all things well" (8:1).

But Sophia does not remain simply a cosmic principle. In Proverbs, we hear that she "builds her house" among us, prepares her great feast and invites the simple and humble to her table, saying: "Come eat of my bread and drink of the wine I have mixed" (Prv 9:1–5). In Baruch, we are told how she "appeared on earth and lived with humankind" (Bar 3:37). In Sirach, we find Sophia seeking a resting place on earth, and the Creator commanding her to pitch her tent and make her home in Jerusalem (Sir 24:3–11). There she offers her invitation: "Come to me, all you who desire me, and eat your fill of my fruits.... Those who eat of me will hunger for more, and those who drink of me will thirst for more" (Sir 24:19–20). In the Wisdom of Solomon, too, Sophia does not remain aloof, but comes among us to make us friends of God: "In every generation she passes into holy souls and makes them friends of God and prophets; for God loves nothing so much as the person who lives with wisdom" (Wis 7:27–28).

2. The early Christian community proclaimed that Wisdom has made her home among us in Jesus of Nazareth.

The ancient Wisdom literature saw Sophia as one who was intimately involved with the whole work of creation, who has now made her home among us and invited us to eat and drink at her table. In Sirach and Baruch, it is clear that Sophia come among us is identified with God's gift of the Torah (Sir 24:23; Bar 4:1). In the Wisdom of Solomon, Sophia is present to human beings in other ways. They can find her "sitting at the gate" in the morning. She "graciously appears to them in their paths and meets them in every thought" (Wis 6:12–16).

Just as some faithful Jewish thinkers interpreted Wisdom making her home among us in terms of God's self-revelation through the Torah, so other (Christian) Jewish believers saw Wisdom as God's self-revelation in Jesus of Nazareth. For these Christians, the image of Sophia who was with God in

creation and who has now pitched her tent among us provided a model for the interpretation of Jesus.

In Luke, Jesus is understood as a child of Wisdom (Lk
7:35) and as a prophet of Wisdom (Lk 11:49). It is Jesus who
does the compassionate deeds of Wisdom: "The blind
receive their sight, the lame walk, the lepers are cleansed, the
deaf hear, the dead are raised, the poor have good news
brought to them" (Lk 7:22). Like Wisdom, Jesus is the Son
who is known by the Father and who knows and reveals the
Father (Lk 10:21–22). He is the one who desires to gather the
children of Jerusalem together as a hen gathers her brood
under her wing (Lk 13:34). In Matthew, Jesus is more clearly
Wisdom herself. Jesus *is* the Wisdom of God who is justified
by her deeds (Mt 11:19). It is Jesus-Wisdom who sends the
prophets (Mt 23:24). It is Jesus, echoing the language of
Sirach, who cries out: "Come to me, all of you that are weary
and are carrying heavy burdens, and I will give you rest.
Take my yoke upon you, and learn from me; for I am gentle
and humble of heart, and you will find rest for your souls.
For my yoke is easy and my burden light" (Mt 11:28–30). In
John, the portrait of Jesus is drawn in terms that echo the
Wisdom tradition, above all in the concept of the Word's
descent to dwell among us, the great "I am" statements, the
"living water" theme of John 4 and the "bread of life" theme
of John 6. Raymond Brown says that, in John's Gospel, Jesus
is "personified Wisdom" and "incarnate Wisdom."[23]

3. *The most radical expression of Wisdom come among us is
found in Paul's identification of divine wisdom with the crucified
one.*

In the context of disputes at Corinth, Paul proclaims his
own theology of true wisdom: "For Jews demand signs and

Greeks desire wisdom, but we proclaim Christ crucified, a stumbling block to Jews and foolishness to Gentiles, but to those who are called, both Jews and Greeks, Christ the power of God and the wisdom of God" (1 Cor 1:22–24). This crucified one, this extreme expression of human vulnerability, Paul tells us, *is* the power of God. This apparent foolishness *is* divine wisdom. The Pauline structure of thought is that the wisdom of God, which is already revealed to us in the wonder of creation, is now revealed in a staggering way in the cross of Jesus. This structure is made explicit when Paul says: "For since, in the wisdom of God, the world did not know God through wisdom, God decided through the foolishness of our proclamation, to save those who believe" (1 Cor 1:21). Jerome Murphy-O'Connor comments that Paul is saying that, in the light of humanity's failure to accept the insight into God offered by wisdom already displayed in creation, "God just went ahead and did something really foolish."[24]

Paul continues: "For God's foolishness is wiser than human wisdom, and God's weakness is stronger than human strength" (1:25). What is this "foolishness" of God? It seems clear that Paul means the foolishness of love beyond understanding. It is the foolishness of divine compassion's vulnerability. Paul's theology of wisdom confronts us with the fact that this wisdom at work in the universe is now revealed in the vulnerable love expressed in the crucified one. A Wisdom Christology that is faithful to Paul's insight will hold together Dante's "love that moves the stars," the love revealed in the universe in all its manifestations, with the shocking depths of divine love's compassion for a suffering world revealed in the cross of Jesus.

An evolutionary Christology will see the evolution of

life and consciousness as the work of divine Wisdom. Our universe expands and unfolds in and through Wisdom. The diversity of life on Earth emerges through evolutionary process and all of this occurs in divine Wisdom. Each creature is in some way the self-expression of divine Wisdom. But Paul's theology keeps before us the confronting idea that divine Wisdom, at work creatively and continuously in the expanding universe and in our evolutionary history, stands revealed above all in the vulnerability and "foolishness" of the cross. This brings to mind again what I have discussed earlier, that there is a freely chosen self-emptying (a divine *kenosis*) and a self-limitation in God's engagement with creation. It is the self-emptying and self-limitation of love.

4. *In the light of the resurrection experience, the early church could come to say that all things are created* **in** *Jesus the Wisdom of God.*

What is the relationship of Jesus to the process of evolution? Ian Barbour has said we can think of Jesus Christ as "representing a new stage in evolution and a new stage in God's activity."[25] I think that Karl Rahner's insights are helpful in developing this line of thought. First, from side of evolving creation, Jesus can be seen as the self-transcendence of the universe into God. Second, from the side of God, Jesus can be seen as God's self-giving to the evolving universe.

This role of Jesus in evolution can be further specified in the light of the biblical tradition that sees Jesus-Wisdom as the one in whom all things were created. It seems that soon after the experience of the resurrection, early Christian communities sang hymns in which Jesus was celebrated in concepts and language that echoed the hymns to Sophia. Remnants of these hymns are found throughout the Christian Scriptures. For example, in the opening of Hebrews we find: "He is the reflection of God's glory and the exact imprint of God's very being, and he sustains all things by his powerful word" (Heb 1:3). In John's Gospel, we read: "In the beginning was the Word, and the Word was with God and the word was God.... All things came into being through him, and without him not one thing came into being.... And the Word became flesh and lived among us, and we have seen his glory" (Jn 1:1–14). And in the great hymn of Colossians we hear: "He is the image of the invisible God, the firstborn of all creation, for in him all things in heaven and earth were created.... All things have been created through him and for him. He himself is before all things, and in him all things hold together.... For in him all the fullness of God was pleased to dwell, and through him God was pleased to reconcile to himself all things, whether on earth or in heaven, by making peace through the blood of his cross" (Col 1:15–20).

The standard biblical commentaries point out that while these texts do not refer explicitly to Jesus as Wisdom, an implicit understanding of Jesus as Wisdom stands behind them. This same kind of implicit identification seems to be behind Paul's attribution of a cosmic role to Jesus Christ in 1 Corinthians: "For us there is one God, the Father, from whom are all things and for whom we exist, and one Lord, Jesus Christ, through whom are all things and through whom we exist" (8:6). Once Jesus is identified with divine Wisdom, then Jesus as divine Wisdom can be understood as the one in whom all things are created. The identification of Jesus with Sophia points simultaneously toward a cosmic Christology and a theology of preexistence and incarnation.

In the light of biological evolution, what does it mean to say that all things are created "in" Jesus the Wisdom of God? First, it suggests a close relationship between creation and incarnation. It suggests that God's self-communication in creation is always directed toward the incarnation. Second, it suggests that everything that comes to be in our evolutionary history is an expression of the abundance that is already in some way in Divine Wisdom. It is as if Wisdom were the template for all that comes to be. Each creature in its own way gives expression to Divine Wisdom. This was certainly the position developed by Bonaventure. Within the trinitarian life, he teaches, the Word is the perfect self-expression of God. The Word of God is the "divine art," *ars suprema, ars Patris.*[26] Bonaventure talks of the Word as the Wisdom of God, who bears in her womb the eternal thoughts of God.[27] All things are found in divine Sophia in unity, and insofar as individual creatures exist they exist because of the distinct divine intention to express them.

Bonaventure sees every creature as "a reflection of divine Wisdom," although each is a reflection "mingled with darkness." The reflection of the eternal Wisdom in creatures is like "a ray of sunshine which penetrates through the window panes breaking up into many colors."[28] In another place, Bonaventure talks about the "many-colored Wisdom of God" radiating forth as from a "marvelous mirror that contains all forms and light, and as from a book in which all stand recorded in accordance with the unfathomable mysteries of God."[29] All creatures are the work of art produced by divine Wisdom. He tells us that "every creature is of its very nature a likeness and resemblance to eternal wisdom."[30]

It seems to me that Bonaventure's insight may be a helpful way of seeing evolution unfolding "in" Christ.

Evolution is the unfolding of the potentialities that are in matter. Bonaventure would say that all these possibilities are "already" in divine Wisdom, the Exemplar, but have to come to be in their specific creaturely uniqueness in the realm of creation. As I have said earlier, contemporary science points to the *chance* that is at the heart of evolution. The rich insight of Bonaventure needs to be understood today in terms of the real unpredictability and novelty of evolutionary change. Wisdom is present in every cosmic event as pattern, archetype, and innovative possibility. But, in the light of our current understanding of evolution, the art of divine Wisdom is not to be thought of as if it were the unfolding of a completely predetermined and predictable plan.

As I pointed out in chapter 3, what must be held together is God's capacity to achieve God's purposes and the integrity of the process of evolution. God's purposes are achieved, not in spite of, but *in and through* the indeterminacy that is built into the process. In this view God would not be understood as another factor operating alongside natural selection, or in addition to it, but as operating through it. This means that divine Wisdom would be understood as working purposefully in and through the chance and lawfulness of biological evolution. Wisdom can work artfully in the unpredictability and "freedom" of nature. In this view, every step along the way, every probing mutation, every adaptation, would occur "in" Wisdom. The divine art would be understood to be at work in our world, working creatively and respectfully with the laws of nature, and with what unfolds through chance and lawfulness in natural selection.

5. *In the resurrection, Jesus-Wisdom becomes a power of trans-formation for the whole of creation.*

We are told in the great hymn of Colossians not only that "all things" are *created* in Jesus Christ, but that "all things" are to be *reconciled* in him. Jesus Christ, Wisdom made flesh, is not simply the self-transcendence of the universe into God, and God's self-communication to the world. He is not simply the one in whom all things were created. A Wisdom Christology, in so far as it takes seriously this text from Colossians and other Christian texts (including Rom 8:21 and Eph 1:10, 20–23), goes further to make the assertion: Jesus of Nazareth, risen from the dead, is the dynamic power at the heart of cosmic processes.

How might this be understood? Christian faith in the resurrection of Jesus affirms not only an event in us (a subjective dimension) but also an event in Jesus Christ (an objective dimension). This transforming event in Jesus can be understood as an event in which the humanity of Jesus is taken into a new relation with divine Wisdom's work in the whole of creation. The Wisdom of God has always been at work, enabling each creature to be and to become. In Jesus risen, a specific human being is radically united with the power of divine Wisdom at work in the universe. In the resurrection, Jesus of Nazareth becomes the Cosmic Christ. The humanity of Christ achieves a new relation with the material universe in the resurrection. The resurrection involves this humanity in Wisdom's cosmic work. Jesus is in this way the first fruits of the new creation.

A sentence of Rahner's captures these ideas: "When the vessel of his body was shattered in death, Christ was poured out over all the cosmos; he became actually, in his very humanity, what he had always been in his dignity, the innermost center of creation."[31] Jesus-Wisdom, risen from the dead, is the irrevocable promise and reality of salvation at work within the evolving universe. This is close to Teilhard's idea of "Christification" of matter, when Teilhard writes "the divine immensity has transformed itself for us into the omnipresence of Christification."[32] The humanity of Jesus is assumed into the life of the trinitarian God, and participates in the divine creative and redemptive presence to all things. Jesus risen has a new bodily relation with the material universe.

6. *The world is a Sacrament of Divine Wisdom—Wisdom Christology as ecological theology.*

I pointed out earlier that, according to Bonaventure, the eternal Wisdom of God is reflected in the great variety of creatures, like "a ray of sunshine, which penetrates through the window panes breaking up into many colors." Each creature can be considered to be a work of art produced by divine Wisdom. Bonaventure sees every creature pointing back to its Creator:

> Therefore, whoever is not enlightened by such great splendor in created things is blind; whoever remains unheedful of such great outcries is deaf; whoever does not praise God in all these effects is dumb; whoever does not turn to the First Principle after so many signs is a fool. Open your eyes, therefore; alert the ears of your spirit, unlock your lips, and apply your heart that you may see, hear, praise, love and adore, magnify and honor your God in every creature, lest perchance, the entire universe rise up against you.[33]

For Bonaventure the diversity and variety of creatures all give expression to the Word and Wisdom of God. For the biblical wisdom tradition too, creatures point back to the one who made them. In the Wisdom of Solomon, we are told:

> For all people who were ignorant of God were foolish by nature; and they were unable from the good things that are seen to know the one who exists, nor did they recognize the artisan while paying heed to his works.... For from the greatness and beauty of created things comes a corresponding perception of their Creator. (Wis 13:1, 5)

The diversity of life on Earth, interconnected and interdependent in the one biosphere of our planet, is a sacrament of divine Wisdom. It gives expression to and manifests Wisdom. It points to the divine artisan. And what it points to is really present in the manifestation. The divine artisan is not only manifested in the beauty and diversity of a tropical rain forest, but is also present to each creature of the forest as the creative power which enables it to be. Creation is a *sacrament* of the divine presence.

If each creature is the self-expression of divine Wisdom, then this points to an ethics of "intrinsic value." The value of things comes not simply from their value to human beings. Things have value in themselves because they are the self-expression of God. They have intrinsic value. They are the created articulation of the eternal Word, divine Wisdom, the Art of God. Birds, plants, forests, mountains, and galaxies have value in themselves because they exist and are held in being by the divine Persons-in-Mutual-Communion, and because they are fruitful expressions of divine Wisdom. They are indeed the voice of the divine, and to destroy one of them irresponsibly is to destroy arbitrarily a mode of divine self-expression. As Thomas Berry has said, "We should be clear about what happens when we destroy the living forms of this planet. The first consequence is that we destroy modes of divine presence." [34]

Christian discipleship is an invitation to contribute creatively to the ongoing process of cultural evolution. Evolution on our planet has entered into a new crucial stage—that of human cultural evolution (Teilhard's "noosphere"). The existence of life as we know it will depend on how the human community responds to the demands of cultural evolution. Teilhard was certainly right in his vision of the church as an essential "phylum of love" within cultural evolution. The church is a Wisdom community committed to the way of Jesus. But the phylum of love is wider than the church. It is as wide as all the ways in which the Reign of God is already at work in our world. It involves all of those who knowingly or unknowingly do the work of Wisdom. It includes all those who build the sense of kinship among the creatures of the God who is Persons-in-Mutual-Love.

Conclusion

THIS BOOK HAS BEEN AN ATTEMPT to articulate a theology of God, one that stands in the Christian tradition but also engages with the insights and challenges offered by evolutionary biology.

I have suggested that at the most fundamental level, God is to be understood as a God of mutual and equal relations. God is a God of mutual friendship, of diversity in unity. Dynamic Being-in-Relation is the very being of God. If God is Being-in-Relation, then this provides a basis for thinking about reality as radically relational. A relational ontology provides a meeting point between Christian theology and evolutionary biology. In a Christian theology, the relational trinitarian God can be understood as making space within the divine relations for a dynamically unfolding universe and for the evolution of life in all its diversity and interconnectedness.

To human observers, the evolution of life through random mutation and natural selection can seem not only glorious and wonderful in its diversity and abundance, but also capricious and cruel. Why would a good and all-powerful God create in such a way? I have suggested that part of the answer to this question is that God is *not* to be seen as absolutely all-powerful, but rather as a relational God who is self-limited by love and respect for finite creatures. Such a God respects not only the freedom of beloved human beings, but also the physical processes of the universe. This God works in and through the laws of nature and in and through the randomness of the process. More and more it would seem that a degree of randomness is essential for the creation of a universe anything like the one we have. God can be understood as the divine artist, achieving the divine purposes by working creatively and adventurously through the laws of nature and through chance.

The theology of original sin and grace needs to take account of biological evolution. Some of the tendencies and drives that were formerly understood as springing from original sin may now be attributed to the genetic predispositions that we share with our early human and prehuman ancestors. Original sin itself can be understood as a universal part of the human condition, by which the history of human rejection of God from the beginning enters into the inner place of our free decisions. With regard to grace, we can think of our forebears as coming to self-consciousness in a world that was not only threatening, but also already a world of grace, a world in which God was already there in self-offering love as a constitutive dimension of human existence in the world. The creation of each human as a spiritual being can be thought of as individual, unique, and personal, but at the same time brought about through God's one divine act of continuous creation.

How are the divine trinitarian Persons related to this ongoing work of creation through biological evolution? I have suggested that the Holy Spirit can be understood as the Life-Giver, the one who is the power of becoming at the heart of evolution, the interior presence of God to all creatures and one who is the ecstatic bringer of communion. Jesus the Wisdom of God is the one in whom all things are created and in whom all will be reconciled, the self-transcendence of the universe into God and God's self-giving to the universe. The Unoriginate Origin in the Trinity, the one who is Father and Mother, is the ultimate Source of all being and all life, the Fountain Fullness from which all things spring. I have suggested that these roles can be understood as distinct and proper to each Person, and I have also argued that because of the divine *koinōnia* and the unity of the divine nature, where one Person acts, the whole Trinity acts.

If God's being is communion, friendship beyond comprehension, then this is what grounds the connectedness of all things in our universe. It is this divine community that constitutes reality as it is and as it becomes. It is divine love that enfolds all creatures and enables them to be. It is this sheer relationality, this communion in diversity, which sustains and empowers biological evolution. This trinitarian constitution of reality calls for human communities based on mutual and equal relations, and on respect for otherness and diversity. It calls human beings to an ecological consciousness, to an empathy for and solidarity with all the life forms of our planet.

Notes

1. INTRODUCTION: EVOLUTION AND GOD

[1]Ian Barbour, *Religion in an Age of Science* (San Francisco: HarperSanFrancisco, 1990), 26–28. Doctrinal reformulation fits within the "theology of nature" approach in Barbour's typology.

[2]See Francisco J. Ayala, "Darwin's Revolution," in John H. Campbell and J. William Schopf (eds.), *Creative Evolution?!* (Boston: Jones & Bartlett, 1994), 1–17.

[3]Charles Darwin, *On the Origin of Species* (London: Unit Library, 1902), 76.

[4]See Motoo Kimura, *The Neutral Theory of Molecular Evolution* (Cambridge: Cambridge University Press, 1983).

[5]See N. Eldredge and S. J. Gould, "Punctuated Equilibria: An Alternative to Phyletic Gradualism," in T. J. M. Schopf (ed.), *Models in Paleobiology* (San Francisco: Freeman, Cooper and Company, 1972), 82–115, and S. J. Gould and N. Eldredge, "Punctuated Equilibrium Comes of Age," *Nature* 366 (1993): 223–27.

[6]B.C.E. (before the common era) and C.E. (common era) are used as alternative labels for dates to B.C. and A.D.

[7]This theology of the divine image is not without its problems. For two helpful approaches to this theme from an ecological and feminist perspective, see Anne M. Clifford, "When Human Beings Become Truly Earthly: An Ecofeminist Proposal for Solidarity," in Ann O'Hara Graff (ed.), *In the Embrace of God: Feminist Approaches to Theological Anthropology* (Maryknoll, N.Y.: Orbis Press, 1995), 173–89, and Mary Catherine Hilkert, "Cry Beloved Image: Rethinking the Image of God" in the same volume, 190–205.

[8]The language used here is undeniably harsh. To "have dominion" translates the Hebrew verb *radah*, which is an expression usually associated with a king's rule (1 Kgs 5:3; Ps 72:8; Ps 110:2; Is 14:6; Ez 34:4). The word *subdue* translates *kabas*, which means literally "to trample under one's feet" (Jer 34:11–16; Zec 9:15; Neh 5:5; 2 Chr 28:10). In the light of the ecological crisis we face today, this is

dangerous language. In its original context it would have had a different impact. The creation stories of the surrounding peoples depicted human beings as slaves who were created to bear the yoke of the gods. Nature itself was understood as dangerous, full of malevolent spirits. In *this* context, the Genesis story tells us that the human vocation is the "kingly" one, of bringing human work and ingenuity to bear on the land. Human beings are called to care for herds, to help grow crops, and to build cities. In a Jewish world, this kingly work was understood in terms of God's compassionate rule. Richard Clifford has argued that the use of *subdue* means to establish a territory in which a life that is faithful to God can be lived: "It does not mean to exploit it but rather to receive it as a gift and live on it." See his "Genesis 1–3: Permission to Exploit Nature?" *Bible Today* (1988): 136. Genesis 1:26–28 needs to be read alongside the command in Genesis 2:15 "to cultivate and to care for" the garden of creation, and alongside the rainbow covenant that God establishes with all living creatures in Genesis 9:12. The biblical language of domination and subduing cannot be used legitimately to justify the ruthless exploitation of the Earth's resources today. We need to recognize the time-conditioned nature of these words and their danger. We also need to hold on to the truth they represent—that human beings are called to cooperate with God in the unfolding of the potentialities of nature.

⁹*Dogmatic Constitution on Divine Revelation* (*Dei Verbum*), 11.

2. THE GOD OF EVOLUTION AS A
GOD OF MUTUAL FRIENDSHIP

¹See Philip Hefner, *The Human Factor: Evolution, Culture and Religion* (Minneapolis: Fortress, 1993), 208–9. For Gerd Theissen's views, see his *Biblical Faith: An Evolutionary Approach* (London: SCM, 1984).

²See, for example, Valerie Saiving Goldstein, "The Human Situation: A Feminine View," *Journal of Religion* 40 (1960): 100–112; Judith Plaskow, *Sex, Sin and Grace: Women's Experience and the Theologies of*

Reinhold Niebuhr and Paul Tillich (New York: University of America, 1980); Susan Nelson Dunfee, "The Sin of Hiding," *Soundings* LXV (1982): 316–27. More recent theologies of sin include Mary Potter Engel, "Evil, Sin and the Violation of the Vulnerable," in Susan Brooks Thistlethwaite and Mary Potter Engel (eds.), *Lift Every Voice: Constructing Christian Theologies from the Underside* (San Francisco: Harper and Row, 1990), 152–64; Delores Williams, "A Womanist Perspective on Sin," in Emily M. Townes (ed.), *A Troubling in My Soul: Womanist Perspectives on Evil and Suffering* (Maryknoll, N.Y.: Orbis Books, 1993), 130–39; Sally Ann Reynolds and Ann Graff, "Sin: When Women Are the Context," in Ann O'Hara Graff (ed.), *In the Embrace of God: Feminist Approaches to Theological Anthropology* (Maryknoll, N.Y.: Orbis, 1995), 161–72.

[3]For a summary of this theme, see Raymond E. Brown, *The Gospel According to John I–XII* (Garden City, N.Y.: Doubleday, 1966), 510–11. For an extended treatment from a feminist perspective, see Dorothy A. Lee, "Abiding in the Fourth Gospel: A Case Study in Feminist Biblical Theology," *Pacifica* 10 (1997): 123–36.

[4]John of Damascus, *De Fide Orthodoxa*, 1.8. John has borrowed freely from an unknown theologian, who is usually called Pseudo-Cyril. See Pseudo-Cyril, *De Sacrosancta Trinitate*, 10 and 23 (*PG*, 77, 1144D and 1164B).

[5]For a critical edition of Richard's *De Trinitate*, see Jean Ribaillier, *Richard de Saint-Victor, De Trinitate, texte critique avec introduction, notes et tables* (Paris: Vrin, 1958). The important Book III has been translated by Grover A. Zinn in *Richard of St. Victor: The Twelve Patriarchs, the Mystical Ark, Book Three of the Trinity* (New York: Paulist Press, 1979).

[6]See Yves Congar, *I Believe in the Holy Spirit, Vol. 1: The Experience of the Spirit* (New York: Seabury Press, 1983), 87.

[7]Sally McFague, *Models of God: Theology for an Ecological, Nuclear Age* (Philadelphia: Fortress Press, 1987), 172.

[8]Elizabeth Johnson, *She Who Is: The Mystery of God in Feminist Theological Discourse* (New York: Crossroad, 1992), 217.

[9]Ibid., 218.

[10]Richard Dawkins, *River Out of Eden: A Darwinian View of Life* (London: Phoenix, 1995), 52.

[11]John Zizioulas, *Being as Communion: Studies in Personhood and the Church* (Crestwood, N.Y.: St. Vladimir's Seminary Press, 1985), 17.

[12]Ibid. See also John Zizioulas, "The Doctrine of the Holy Trinity: The Significance of the Cappadocian Contribution," in Christoph Schwobel (ed.), *Trinitarian Theology Today* (Edinburgh: T & T Clark, 1995), 44–60.

[13]Walter Kasper, *The God of Jesus Christ* (New York: Paulist Press, 1976), 310. See also p. 290.

[14]Catherine LaCugna, *God for Us: The Trinity and Christian Life* (San Francisco: HarperSanFrancisco, 1991), 250.

[15]Ibid., 310.

[16]See also Kasper, *God of Jesus Christ*, 290 and 320. Anthony Kelly's theology of the Trinity as divine Being-in-Love would lend support to this line of thought. See *The Trinity of Love: A Theology of the Christian God* (Wilmington, Del.: Michael Glazier, 1989). See also Colin Gunton's trinitarian principles of freedom-contingency, relation and energy, which he suggests apply in science, in *The Promise of Trinitarian Theology* (Edinburgh: T & T Clark, 1991), 142–61.

[17]On this concept of creaturely communion as communion by participation, see Zizioulas, *Being as Communion*, 94.

[18]Hans Urs von Balthazar, *Theo-Drama: Theological Dramatic Theory, Vol. IV: The Action* (San Francisco: Ignatius Press, 1994), 327.

[19]*Theo-Drama: Theological Dramatic Theory, Vol. 1: Prolegomena* (San Francisco: Ignatius Press, 1988), 20.

[20]See John O'Donnell, *Hans Urs von Balthasar* (Collegeville: Liturgical Press, 1992) 139–53.

[21]I have discussed Bonaventure's theology as a foundation for a contemporary ecological theology in *Jesus the Wisdom of God: An Ecological Theology* (Maryknoll, N.Y.: Orbis Books, 1995), 101–30.

[22]*1 Sent.* d.2, a.u., q.2.

[23]See *1 Sent.* d.6, a.u., q.1–3; *Breviloqium*, 1, 8.

[24]Jurgen Moltmann, *The Trinity and the Kingdom of God: The Doctrine of God* (London: SCM, 1981), 109–10. Moltmann connects his thought at this point with the Jewish doctrine of *zimzum*, developed by Isaac Luria.

[25]Johnson, *She Who Is*, 234–35.

[26]Stephen Happel, "Divine Providence and Instrumentality," in Robert John Russell, Nancey Murphy, and Arthur R. Peacocke (eds.), *Chaos and Complexity* (Vatican City: Vatican Observatory Publications, 1995), 200.

[27]William R. Stoeger, "Describing God's Action in the World in Light of Scientific Knowledge of Reality," in Russell, et al. (eds.), *Chaos and Complexity*, 256–57.

[28]As Mary Catherine Hilkert has pointed out, it transforms our notion of what it means to be made in the image of God: "The mystery of what it is to be a human person and what constitutes authentic human, social, and political relationships is grounded in the deeper mystery of God: At the heart of reality is relationship, personhood, communion. The trinitarian foundation of all of reality calls for human societies that are characterized by mutuality, interdependence, inclusiveness, equality and freedom.... While the dignity of every human person needs to be respected and protected, human persons do not image God primarily as individuals, but rather in 'right relationships' with one another. The image of God is reflected most clearly in communities characterized by equality, respect for differences and uniqueness, and mutual love" ("Cry Beloved Image: Rethinking the Image of God," in Ann O'Hara Graff (ed.), *In the Embrace of God*, 200).

3. THE GOD OF EVOLUTION AS A
GOD OF FREE SELF-LIMITATION IN LOVE

[1]For a helpful overview of a "self-limiting" theology of God in relation to other ways of connecting God and nature see Ian Barbour, *Religion in an Age of Science* (San Francisco: HarperSanFrancisco, 1990), 243–70.

[2]Daniel C. Dennett, *Kind of Minds: Towards an Understanding of Consciousness* (London: Weidenfeld and Nicolson, 1996), 159–60.

[3]Ibid., 164–68.

[4]Jurgen Moltmann, whose work I admire, makes much of the "victims" of evolution in *The Way of Jesus Christ: Christology in Messianic Dimensions* (London: SCM, 1990), 274–341.

[5]John F. Haught, *Science and Religion: From Conflict to Conversation* (New York: Paulist Press, 1995), 60.

[6]For the development of these themes in process theology, see Alfred North Whitehead, *Process and Reality*, corrected edition, ed. D. R. Griffin and D. W. Sherbourne (New York: Free Press, 1929, 1978); Charles Hartshorne, *The Divine Relativity: A Social Conception of God* (New Haven: Yale University Press, 1948 and 1964), and *A Natural Theology for Our Time* (La Salle, Il.: Open Court, 1948 and 1967); John B. Cobb and David R. Griffin, *Process Theology: An Introductory Exposition* (Philadelphia: Westminster Press, 1976). See also Barbour, *Religion in an Age of Science*; Charles Birch, *On Purpose* (Kensington, New South Wales: University Press, 1990), and, for a theology of divine kenosis influenced by process thought, John F. Haught, *Mystery and Promise* (Collegeville: Liturgical Press, 1993).

[7]On these themes see my *Jesus the Wisdom of God: An Ecological Theology* (Maryknoll, N.Y.: Orbis Press, 1995), 122–30. See also the work of Arthur Peacocke, *Theology for a Scientific Age* (Minneapolis: Fortress Press, 1993), 87–183; John Polkinghorne, *Science and Christian Belief* (London: SPCK, 1994), 71–87; Jurgen Moltmann, *God in Creation* (London: SCM, 1985), 185–214; and Ted Peters, *God as Trinity: Relationality and Temporality in Divine Life* (Louisville: Westminster/John Knox Press, 1993), 179–82.

[8]Walter Kasper, *The God of Jesus Christ* (London: SCM, 1983) 194–95.

[9]Lucien Richard, *Christ the Self-Emptying of God* (New York: Paulist Press, 1997), 136.

[10]John Polkinghorne, *Reason and Reality* (London: SPCK, 1991), 84, and *Science and Providence* (London: SPCK, 1989), 66–67.

[11]S. J. Gould, *Wonderful Life: The Burgess Shale and the Nature of History* (London: Penguin Books, 1989), 35.

[12]Stephen Jay Gould, *Life's Grandeur: The Spread of Excellence from Plato to Darwin* (London: Vintage Books, 1996). Gould acknowledges that humans are uniquely complex and that this requires some acknowledgment of a trend (p. 3), but denies that, *overall*, progress exists as a general trend at all (p. 4). He does not deny increased complexity in some species, but sees this as restricted to only a few species, and as an incidental effect rather than as the intended result of evolutionary change (p. 197).

[13]To say that genetic mutations are "random" is not to say that they do not have a cause. Genetic mutations may be caused by a number of factors, including X rays, cosmic rays, radioactive substances, certain chemicals, and "mutator genes." *Random* in this context simply means that there is no general bias toward improvement.

[14]Jacques Monod, *Chance and Necessity* (London: Collins, 1972).

[15]See, for example, Richard Dawkins, *The Blind Watchmaker* (Harlow: Longmans, 1986); Daniel C. Dennett, *Darwin's Dangerous Idea* (London: Allen Lane, 1995).

[16]Ernst Mayr, "Evolution," *Scientific American* 134 (September 1978): 50.

[17]Gould, *Life's Grandeur*, 216. See also p. 175.

[18]Charles Birch is an example of an eminent biologist who finds no difficulty in connecting the randomness in nature with a theological conviction of divine purpose. See his *On Purpose*.

[19]For an example of a physicist who finds direction in the universe, see Paul Davies's *The Cosmic Blueprint* (New York: Simon & Schuster, 1987) and *The Mind of God: Science and the Search for Ultimate Meaning* (London: Simon & Schuster, 1992).

[20]See John D. Barrow and Frank J. Tipler, *The Anthropic Cosmological Principle* (New York: Oxford University Press, 1986).

[21]David J. Bartholomew, *God of Chance* (London: SCM, 1984), 97–98.

[22]Edward Farley, *Divine Empathy: A Theology of God* (Minneapolis: Fortress Press, 1996), 197.

[23]Peacocke, *Theology for a Scientific Age*, 174–77.

[24]Ibid., 175.

[25]Keith Ward, *God, Chance and Necessity* (Oxford: Oneworld, 1996), 80–81.

[26]Ibid., 135. See also p. 77, where Ward distinguishes his view from that of Arthur Peacocke.

[27]See, for example, Karl Rahner, "Freedom. II. Theological," in Karl Rahner (ed.), *Encyclopedia of Theology: A Concise Sacramentum Mundi* (London: Burns and Oates, 1975), 545.

[28]Haught, *Science and Religion*, 63.

[29]Ibid., 67.

4. HUMAN BEINGS BEFORE GOD
IN AN EVOLUTIONARY WORLD

[1]Richard Leakey, *The Origin of Humankind* (London: Phoenix, 1994), xv.

[2]Ibid., xiv.

[3]Ibid., 83.

[4]On the multiregional approach, see M. H. Wolpoff, Wu Xinzhi, and A. Thorne, "Modern *Homo sapiens*' Origins: A General Theory of Hominid Evolution Involving the Fossil Evidence from East Asia," in F. Smith and F. Spencer (eds.), *The Origins of Modern Humans: A World Survey of the Fossil Evidence* (New York: Alan Liss, 1984), 411–83, and A. Thorne and M. Wolpoff, "The Multiregional Evolution of Humans," *Scientific American* (April 1992): 28–33.

[5]Chris Stringer and Robin McKie, *African Exodus: The Origins of Modern Humanity* (London: Pimlico, 1996), 155.

[6]Leakey, *Origin of Humankind*, 99.

[7]There is no doubt that this scientific picture will develop and change. But this is no excuse for theology avoiding entering into discussion with evolutionary science. We need to engage with the world picture of our contemporaries, even if it is a tentative one. Theology may well need to be done again when significant new

information challenges an older worldview. In any case, the theological positions I am developing here do not relate to the details
of the picture, but to the broad concept of human evolution.

[8]Many other theologians might be discussed in this context.
Sebastian Moore, for example, sees original sin as the withdrawal
into isolation away from the ultimate mystery that is the source of
all our meaning and value, a withdrawal and refusal which is
stored and expressed in our institutions and cultural achieve-
ments. See *The Fire and the Rose Are One* (London: Darton, Longman and Todd, 1980), 66–70. He also sees the fall in terms of
psychic life, in which there can be an arrest at an early ego stage,
so that the ego of the adult remains compulsively self-securing.
See *Jesus the Liberator of Desire* (New York: Crossroad, 1989), 25–30.
Neil Ormerod has built on some of Moore's insights. He sees original sin as original self-disesteem, a felt rejection of our human
nature prior to the exercise of our freedom. See his *Grace and Dis-
grace* (Newtown, New South Wales: E. J. Dwyer, 1992), 151–62.
Marjorie Hewitt Suchocki argues that original sin should be seen
as rebellion against creatures, with God as the cosufferer in this
rebellion. She finds structures that predispose us to sin in the
human bent toward aggression, the interrelationships of humans
that involve us in a world of violence, and the social structures
that shape and influence us. See *The Fall to Violence: Original Sin in
Relational Theology* (New York: Continuum, 1994).

[9]For Niebuhr's view on this, see Reinhold Niebuhr, *The Nature
and Destiny of Man* (New York: Charles Scribner's Sons, 1941).

[10]Charles Birch and John B. Cobb, *The Liberation of Life: From the
Cell to the Community* (Cambridge: Cambridge University Press,
1981), 120.

[11]Gabriel Daly, *Creation and Redemption* (Dublin: Gill and
Macmillan, 1988), 138.

[12]Ibid., 144–45.

[13]Ibid., 146.

[14]Philip Hefner, *The Human Factor: Evolution, Culture and Religion* (Minneapolis: Fortress, 1993), 132.

[15]Hefner is here following the work of George Edwin Pugh, *The

Biological Origin of Human Values (New York: Basic Books, 1977), 284–88.

[16]Donald T. Campbell, "The Conflict Between Social and Biological Evolution and the Concepts of Original Sin," *Zygon* 10 (1975): 234–49.

[17]Hefner, *Human Factor*, 240.

[18]Karl Rahner, "The Theological Concept of Concupiscentia," *Theological Investigations I* (Baltimore: Helicon Press, 1961), 347–82.

[19]Stephen J. Duffy, *The Dynamics of Grace: Perspectives in Theological Anthropology* (Collegeville: Liturgical Press, 1993), 226.

[20]Karl Rahner, *Foundations of Christian Faith* (New York: Seabury Press, 1978), 106–15.

[21]On this, see Holmes Rolston III, "Does Nature Need to Be Redeemed," *Zygon* 29 (1994): 205–29.

[22]Langdon Gilkey, "Evolution, Culture, and Sin: Responding to Philip Hefner's Proposal," *Zygon* 30 (1995): 305.

[23]On the relationship between ethics and our genetic inheritance, see Francisco J. Ayala, "So Human an Aminal: Evolution and Ethics" in Ted Peters (ed.), *Science and Theology: The New Consonance* (Boulder, Colorado: Westview Press, 1998), 121–136.

[24]Rahner, *Foundations of Christian Faith*, 116.

[25]Leakey, *Origin of Humankind*, 155–56.

[26]This teaching was presented in the pope's encyclical letter *Humani Generis* (1950).

[27]"The Theory of Evolution and the 'Gospel of Life,'" *Catholic International* 8, No. 1 (1997): 14–16. The address was given on October 23, 1996. See *L'Osservatore Romano* (Eng.), October 30, 1996.

[28]Ibid., 15.

[29]Stephen Jay Gould, "Nonoverlapping Magisteria," *Natural History* 106 (March 1997): 16–22.

[30]While I gladly accept the point made by both Pope John Paul II and Stephen Jay Gould about the different competencies and methodologies of science and theology, it is true as well that if theology is to do its task, theology must actively engage with the fruits of

science. John Paul II calls theologians to this task, and this book is an attempt at such a theology. To put it another way, Gould's "nonoverlapping magisteria," important as it is, is only part of the answer with regard to the relationship between theology and science. For an overview of this whole issue see Ian Barbour, *Religion in an Age of Science* (San Francisco: HarperSanFrancisco, 1990), 3–30. See also Ted Peters, "Science and Theology: Toward Consonance," in Peters (ed.), *Science and Theology,* 11–39.

[31]Zoltan Alszeghi, "Development in the Doctrinal Formulations of the Church concerning the Theory of Evolution," *Concilium* 6 (1967): 17.

[32]Michael Schmaus, *Dogma 2: God and Creation* (London: Sheed and Ward, 1969), 135.

[33]Ibid., 135–43.

[34]Karl Rahner, "Evolution: II. Theological," in Karl Rahner (ed.), *Encyclopedia of Theology: A Concise Sacramentum Mundi* (London: Burns and Oates, 1975), 487–88. In recent work, Anne Clifford has suggested a new approach to this issue—that of "Generationism." See her "Biological Evolution and the Human Soul" in Peters (ed.), *Science and Theology,* 162–173.

5. EVOLUTION AND THE HOLY SPIRIT

[1]*On the Holy Spirit*, 1, 3 (translated by Blomfield Jackson in *The Nicene and Post-Nicene Fathers*—henceforth *"NPNF"*—2d Series, 8:3). In this case, I have changed the translation by repeating the words "Glory be to the Father" for the sake of clarity in English. For an introduction to the work of the Cappadocians, see Anthony Meredith, *The Cappadocians* (London: Geoffrey Chapman, 1995).

[2]*On the Holy Spirit*, 6, 13 (*NPNF*, 2d Series, 8:8).

[3]*On the Holy Spirit*, 18, 45 (*NPNF*, 2d Series, 8:28). Basil embraced the distinction between one *ousia* and three hypostases in God, and taught that each hypostasis was distinguished by a special property: fatherhood, sonship, and sanctification. The other Cappadocians define these characteristics as ingenerate-

ness, generateness, and procession *(ekporeusis)*. While in his public teaching Basil, probably out of pastoral sensitivity, refrained from simply saying that the Holy Spirit is God, his friend Gregory of Nazianzus criticized him for this in a letter written in 372/3, and in his fifth *Theological Oration*, boldly asserted: "What, then? Is the Spirit God? Most certainly. Well, then, is he consubstantial? Yes, if he is God."

⁴J. D. Zizioulas, "The Teaching of the Second Ecumenical Council on the Holy Spirit in Historical and Ecumenical Perspective," in J. S. Martin (ed.), *Credo in Spiritum Sanctum,* Vol. 1 (Roma/Vatican City: Libreria Editrice Vaticana, 1983), 39.

⁵Basil, with the East, uses the word *ekporeuesthai* (Jn 15:26) to describe the distinctive procession of the Holy Spirit, whereas in the West *procession* was used as a generic word applicable to both the Word and the Spirit.

⁶*On the Holy Spirit*, 18, 47 (*NPNF*, 2d Series, 8:29).

⁷See Jurgen Moltmann, *The Spirit of Life: A Universal Affirmation* (Minneapolis: Fortress Press, 1992), 289–309; Elizabeth Johnson, *She Who Is: The Mystery of God in Feminist Theological Discourse* (New York: Crossroad, 1992), 124–49.

⁸This is from Letter 38 of Basil, now attributed to Gregory of Nyssa (my translation—see *NPNF*, 2d Series, 8:139).

⁹Karl Rahner has done much to clarify the proper role of the Word in the incarnation. See his *The Trinity* (New York: Herder and Herder, 1970), 27. On the proper role of the Holy Spirit in our sanctification, see David Coffey, "The Gift of the Holy Spirit," *Irish Theological Quarterly* 38 (1971): 202–23 and "A Proper Mission for the Holy Spirit," *Theological Studies* 47 (1986): 227–50; Robert Faricy, "The Trinitarian Indwelling," *The Thomist* 35 (1971): 369–404.

¹⁰See Karl Rahner, *Foundations of Christian Faith* (New York: Seabury Press, 1978), 197.

¹¹The Creed also describes the Holy Spirit as "proceeding" from the Father (Jn 15:26) and as "having spoken through the prophets" (2 Pt 1:21).

[12]*The Hexaemeron*, 2, 6 (*NPNF*, 2d Series, 8:63). I have added the emphasis.

[13]Ibid., 62–63.

[14]Yves Congar also accepts this interpretation: "In Genesis 1:2, the Spirit is shown, in a sense, as God's *ruach* hatching the egg of the World." *I Believe in the Holy Spirit, Vol. III* (New York: Seabury Press, 1983), 161. In a note, Congar refers to Louis Bouyer's *Woman and Man with God* (London: Darton, Longman and Todd, 1960), 189 where Bouyer refers to Jewish exegesis of this text.

[15]See, for example, his article, "Evolution: II. Theological," in Karl Rahner (ed.), *Encyclopedia of Theology: A Concise Sacramentum Mundi* (London: Burns and Oates, 1975), 478–88.

[16]See Rahner's "Christology Within an Evolutionary View of the World," *Theological Investigations 5* (London: Darton, Longman and Todd, 1966), 157–92, and his *Foundations of Christian Faith*, 178–203. See also his *Hominisation: The Evolutionary Origin of Man as a Theological Problem* (New York: Herder and Herder, 1965).

[17]Walter Kasper, *The God of Jesus Christ*, (New York: Paulist Press, 1976), 227.

[18]Rumi, *Mathnawi*, 5, 39. See Yves Congar, *I Believe in the Holy Spirit. Vol. II* (New York: Seabury Press, 1983), 220–21.

[19]Dante, *The Divine Comedy: Paradise*, 33. See Congar, *I Believe in the Holy Spirit, Vol. II*, 221.

[20]See Michael Schmaus, *Dogma 2: God and Creation* (London: Sheed and Ward, 1969), 553.

[21]Moltmann, *The Spirit of Life: A Universal Affirmation* (Minneapolis: Fortress Press, 1992), xi.

[22]Elizabeth A. Johnson, *Women, Earth, and Creator Spirit* (New York: Paulist Press, 1993), 2.

[23]Ibid., 50.

[24]As I have indicated in chapter 2, I think it best to think of creation unfolding *within* God. In this sense, creation is never "outside" God. But what the spatial metaphor "outside" points to in the context of this chapter is undeniably true—that creatures are not God, and that for the Spirit to bring creatures into communion

with God, is to "extend" the divine communion so that it embraces what is not divine. See Christian Duquoc, *Dieu different* (Paris: Cerf, 1977), 121–22. See also Congar, *I Believe in the Holy Spirit, Vol. III*, 148.

[25]Congar, *I Believe in the Holy Spirit: Vol. III*, 144–54.

[26]Ibid., 149.

[27]Ibid., 150.

[28]Moltmann, *Spirit of Life*, 10.

[29]Ibid.

[30]Ibid., 225.

[31]Ibid., 228.

[32]Congar, *I Believe in the Holy Spirit, Vol. III*, 144.

[33]Moltmann uses this phrase, in *Spirit of Life*, 12.

6. EVOLUTION AND JESUS, THE WISDOM OF GOD

[1]Teilhard de Chardin, *The Phenomenon of Man* (London: William Collins, 1959, 1977), 329. Many biologists today would reject the concept of a "law" of increased complexity, although they accept the fact of increased complexity in some species.

[2]Ibid., 202.

[3]Christopher F. Mooney, *Teilhard de Chardin and the Mystery of Christ* (London: Collins, 1964), 65–66.

[4]Ibid., 279–99.

[5]Toward the end of *The Phenomenon of Man*, Teilhard admits that his very concept of the Omega Point is motivated by Christian faith. See p. 322. On "Christ the Evolver" see Teilhard de Chardin, *Science and Christ* (London: Collins, 1968), 164–71.

[6]*Le Milieu divin* (London: Collins, 1960), 112.

[7]Ibid., 115.

[8]"*Le Christ évoluteur*" (1942), quoted in Mooney, *Teilhard de Chardin and the Mystery of Christ*, 106.

[9]"*Ce que le monde attend en ce moment de l'Église de Dieu*" (1952), quoted in Mooney, *Teilhard de Chardin and the Mystery of Christ*, 133.

[10]Karl Rahner, *Foundations of Christian Faith* (New York: Seabury Press, 1978), 179. See Rahner's foundational article "Christology Within an Evolutionary World," in his *Theological Investigations V* (Baltimore: Helicon Press, 1966), 157–92, and his more recent thought on the issue in "Natural Science and Reasonable Faith," in *Theological Investigations XXI* (New York: Crossroad, 1988), 16–55. For my own fuller response to Rahner's evolutionary Christology, see *Jesus and the Cosmos* (New York: Paulist Press, 1991).

[11]Rahner, *Foundations of Christian Faith*, 189.

[12]Ibid., 181.

[13]Ibid., 197.

[14]See, particularly, his *The Crucified God* (New York: Harper and Row, 1974).

[15]Jurgen Moltmann, *The Way of Jesus Christ: Christology in Messianic Dimensions* (London: SCM, 1990), 274–312.

[16]Ibid., 297.

[17]See Moltmann, *Way of Jesus Christ*, 304.

[18]Moltman, *Way of Jesus Christ*, 303.

[19]Ibid., 317.

[20]Ibid., 311.

[21]I think that some of Moltmann's criticisms of Teilhard and, in a particular way, of Rahner are unwarranted. In later essays, Rahner deals with some of the issues that Moltmann accuses him of neglecting. See, for example, "Natural Science and Reasonable Faith," where Rahner discusses the future of matter, and says that, in one's approach to biological evolution, "one must allow for surprises, defective developments, dead ends, for a total halt to progress as such." Christian optimism, Rahner points out, is based not upon evolution itself, but upon God's action in Christ. It is only in Christ that we can affirm "that this world evolution in the phase of its spiritual history is not only capable of arriving at an immediacy to God, but that even now it has entered upon a phase through which…this goal will actually be attained, and that the catastrophe, which in itself is possible, and the total halt to progress, will not come to pass. This irreversibility and this orientation toward a

future goal that will actually be attained, which are characteristic of the world's evolution and its history of freedom, are present for Christians in the Christian dogma of the Jesus Christ as the 'Logos of God made flesh,' as God's irrevocable promise of salvation in Jesus of Nazareth" (p. 55). Rahner clearly has a more critical approach to evolution than Moltmann allows.

[22]I have developed Wisdom Christology in more detail in *Jesus the Wisdom of God: An Ecological Theology* (Maryknoll, N.Y.: Orbis Press, 1995) and attempted to show there its relationship with contemporary feminist Christology and its significance for inter-religious dialogue.

[23]Raymond E. Brown, *The Gospel According to John, I–XII* (Garden City, N.Y.: Doubleday, 1966), cxxii–cxxiv.

[24]Jerome Murphy-O'Connor, *1 Corinthians* (Wilmington, Del.: Michael Glazier, 1979), 14.

[25]Ian Barbour, *Religion in an Age of Science* (San Francisco: HarperSanFrancisco, 1990), 211.

[26]*1 Sent.*, d.6, a.u., q.3, resp.; *Breviloquium*, 1, 8; *Hexaemeron*, 1.

[27]*Hexaemeron*, 20, 5; *Breviloquium*, 8.

[28]*Hexaemeron*, 12, 14–16.

[29]*Lignum vitae*, 46.

[30]"*Omnis enim creatura ex natura est illius aeternae sapientiae quaedam effigies et simultudo*" (*Itinerarium*, 2.12).

[31]Karl Rahner, *On the Theology of Death* (New York: Herder and Herder, 1962), 66.

[32]See chap. 6, n. 6.

[33]*Itinerarium Mentis in Deum*, 1.15. For the translation, see Philotheus Boehner (trans.), *Saint Bonaventure's Itinerarium Mentis in Deum: With an Introduction, Translation and Commentary* (Saint Bonaventure, N.Y.: Franciscan Institute, 1956), 29.

[34]Thomas Berry, *The Dream of the Earth* (San Francisco: Sierra Club Books, 1988), 11.